599. 74428

I've travelled the world twice over,
Met the famous: saints and sinners,
Poets and artists, kings and queens,
Old stars and hopeful beginners,
I've been where no-one's been before,
Learned secrets from writers and cooks
All with one library ticket
To the wonderful world of books.

© Janice James.

The wisdom of the ages
Is there for you and me,
The wisdom of the ages,
In your local library

There's large print books
And talking books,
For those who cannot see,
The wisdom of the ages,
It's fantastic, and it's free.

Written by Sam Wood, aged 92

Books by Gareth Patterson

WITH MY SOUL
AMONGST LIONS

When George Adamson was murdered, Gareth Patterson vowed to continue his work. He successfully cared for and restored George's lion cubs, who were once again orphaned, into the wild. Batian, Furaha and Rafiki became his life's work and he became one of their pride. Gareth prepared them for all the dangers they might face, but unfortunately could never completely guard them from their most lethal enemy — man. Too soon Batian, the pride male, became the victim of a cruel and premeditated murder, leaving the other lions facing equal dangers.

Books by Gareth Patterson
Published by The House of Ulverscroft:

LAST OF THE FREE

GARETH PATTERSON

◆

WITH MY SOUL AMONGST LIONS

A Moving Story of the Struggle
to Protect the Last Adamson Lions

Complete and Unabridged

ULVERSCROFT
Leicester

First published in Great Britain in 1995 by
Hodder and Stoughton Limited
London

First Large Print Edition
published 1997
by arrangement with
Hodder and Stoughton Limited
London

British Library CIP Data

Patterson, Gareth
    With my soul amongst lions: a moving story
    of the struggle to protect the last
    Adamson lions.—Large print ed.—
    Ulverscroft large print series: non-fiction
    1. Patterson, Gareth 2. Wildlife conservationists
    —Africa 3. Lions 4. Wildlife conservation—Africa
    5. Large type books
    I. Title
    639.9'7'974428

    ISBN 0–7089–3740–3

Published by
F. A. Thorpe (Publishing) Ltd.
Anstey, Leicestershire

Set by Words & Graphics Ltd.
Anstey, Leicestershire
Printed and bound in Great Britain by
T. J. Press (Padstow) Ltd., Padstow, Cornwall

This book is printed on acid-free paper

This book is dedicated to Rafiki,
my lion daughter and to God,
who protects her.

Acknowledgements

This is the sequel to *Last of the Free* and the people listed in the Acknowledgements of that book are once again thanked. I wish to emphasise my appreciation to the Government of Botswana and to the many officials who have been supportive and sympathetic to my work.

Special thanks again are due to Rozanne Savory, a steadfast friend who has given me so much support during the past decade of my 'Lion Life'. To Julie, I will never be able to thank you enough for your endurance, love and support for myself and the lions. You must write your story now, of the 'Lion' days and nights we spent together and apart.

I would also like to thank Gloria Keverne for her compassion; my agent Tony Peake for being there and bearing with me; Leanne Wright of Sampson, Okes, Higgins, Chapman Inc for advice; Christel de Wit for her assistance during the difficult time of Press liaising; Bane Sesa, a good and loyal friend; the family members and friends of the late Isaac Mangagola for their kindness, and my editor Dawn Bates and her colleagues at Hodder and Stoughton.

Lastly, to Karin with my love.

Foreword

by Rozanne Savory, Trustee of the Tuli Lion Trust and a long-time friend of a lion man.

I first met Gareth Patterson in 1981 when he was a junior ranger at a private game reserve in the eastern Transvaal in South Africa. We subsequently shared a portion of our lives together in those early days — in the days when his great love of lions began in the Tuli bushlands.

The Tuli bushlands is a harsh place of great beauty and diversity. A place of extremes — a place of intense heat, of wide (mostly dry) rivers, of lush riverine bush, of wide open plains, of rocky outcrops and occasional baobab trees, a dry place prone to drought where great elephant herds roam. A place of extremes which you grow to love. In those early days (1983), the Tuli bushlands was also a place of lion prides. Over the years, and as Gareth had always predicted, those lion prides have disappeared. Pride structures have disintegrated, and lions only in small groups, or as individuals, occur today.

The last Adamson lioness, Rafiki, is one of those lions. She lives in the Tuli bushlands with her son and her daughter.

This book, Gareth's fifth, is the sequel to *Last of the Free. Last of the Free* was full of hope. It told the story of the Adamson lions' introduction to the Tuli bushlands and of their successful rehabilitation into the wilds. Batian, Furaha and Rafiki adopted the Tuli as their new home. They became integrated into it, securing their own territories, mating with wild lions and becoming completely independent and free.

Tragedy struck when the courageous and beautiful male lion, Batian, inadvertently ventured into South Africa and was shot dead.

Over time, the period of hope changed to a time of pain and sorrow. Batian's death was the beginning. Gareth and his girlfriend, Julie, had enormous courage, but the odds were always stacked against them.

I was one of the few privileged people who was allowed to stay at Tawana Camp with Gareth and Julie. Many times I have seen Gareth with the lions and always it was an emotional experience. I knew I was witnessing something extraordinary. I have heard him calling across the Tuli bushlands in the early evening. I have heard the lions responding. I have watched the greeting ceremony where Gareth became part of the pride, where nothing else in the world mattered to him. I have seen the love between man and beast. I will never forget it.

Life at Tawana Camp was incredibly hard. It was mostly terribly hot and dry. There was no running water. Equipment quickly showed signs of wear. The sun, the dust and the occasional downpour took their toll. Vehicles constantly needed attention. There was little money for anything. And always, there were the promises of funding and assistance, but they seldom came to anything. So often, people just wanted to meet 'The Lion Man' so that they could talk about him at their cocktail parties. Their promises were hollow, and Gareth and Julie's hopes were dashed — time and again.

I have watched as the sequence of events documented both in *Last of the Free* and in this book have unfolded. I have felt so much of Gareth and Julie's pain and disappointment, both at the time, and again while typing this manuscript where I have often stopped to cry. I have, perhaps more than anyone else, been kept in touch with events as they happened.

Gareth is a man of passion. He is a man of strong character, sincerity and determination. He has a certain arrogance, but yet is sympathetic and compassionate, and something which touches him emotionally will make him cry unashamedly. He is a man who can inflame a rage in you one minute, but who can awaken a protective and loving response in you the next. A fascinating and magnetic man. Life with Gareth is not an easy one, but nor is it dull.

The unassuming and ever generous hero in this book is Julie. Julie's courage and inner strength, her support and love both for Gareth and the lions are evident. Always there, always putting Gareth and the lions first and knowing only too well that Gareth's concern for the wellbeing of the lions was paramount. It took precedence over everything else. In the end, the unrelenting emotional stresses and physical hardships of life in the Tuli bushlands became too much. She left the area and all its ghosts — the ghosts of the lions which were no more, and perhaps too the ghost of her love for Gareth.

I visited Gareth at the original 'old' Tawana camp one Christmas while Julie was spending some time with her family in South Africa. I took with me all kinds of special things to eat. On my first evening, Christmas Eve, the lions arrived at camp. Gareth wanted to give them 'something' at Christmas, and he did. All the steak and eggs I'd brought with me. Such was his love for his lions. They came first. They always will.

ROZANNE SAVORY

Author's Note

With my Soul Amongst Lions tells of the most recent chapter in the story of the remaining Adamson lions, and is the sequel to *Last of the Free*. In *Last of the Free*, I related how, after the murder of the Grand Old Lion Man of Africa, George Adamson, I, an admirer and colleague, adopted his last three lion orphans. There was Batian, the male, Furaha and Rafiki, the two sisters. I told how I moved the young lions out of the volatile 'shifta'-plagued Kora National Reserve, George's home for nineteen years, and restored them to the wilds thousands of kilometres south in the Botswana Tuli bushlands — my own wilderness home. There I lived in the wilds with the lions and my girlfriend, Julie Davidson.

In the previous book, I told of my early adventures with the lions and how, with them, I lived, hunted, played and rested as they quickly progressed towards their ultimate freedom, independence and important securing of their own territory.

Living as a human member of a lion pride, I had a unique, unparalleled opportunity of experiencing life in the wilds through lions' eyes. Initially, I was their protector. Then came the day they saved my life. A leopard charged towards me and as it was about to make its final pounce, Furaha leapt over and across me, slamming into the leopard — and later, with her brother and sister, killed my attacker.

Last of the Free ended as this story begins — with the murder by South African hunters of my beloved male lion, Batian. He was like a first-born son to Julie and me. In *With my Soul Amongst Lions*, I continue the story from that time to the present. Three harsh gruelling years which never would I wish to re-live, but in a sense, by writing this book, I have. In many ways, I did not wish to relate this story as much of that time was emotionally harrowing and while writing, many of these emotions re-surfaced.

I tell of Julie and my continued efforts to give greater protection to lions and all wildlife of the Tuli bushlands — a privately owned wildlife area at the junction of Botswana, Zimbabwe and South Africa. Our efforts involved confronting factors such as harsh daily conditions, poaching, illegal hunting, lack of funding and complicated human politics. The time took its toll on my relationship with Julie and this became yet another casualty of our work. The struggle in the bushlands culminated in a time of death: death of a man, the death of lions, suspected murder, dark dealings and fears for our own lives . . . resulting, in turn, in my solitary struggle to maintain freedom for those who are the focus of my life — the lions, and one in particular.

WITH MY SOUL
AMONGST LIONS

The future creeps slowly towards one,
the present is arrowswift, and
I have learnt the past haunts
being forever motionless

My soul was amongst lions,
then the veils of pain and loss
were to be hung by fate
upon my face

The veils, like unwelcomed
   companions
cling still as I write these words,
but may slip away and fall
at the story's end . . .
Leaving me clean, free at last,
with my soul amongst lions.

19 October 1994:
Written today for tomorrow

Prologue

THE four men were prepared, sitting armed in perverse anticipation — they awaited the appearance of a lion. The donkey, shot earlier as a bait, hung heavily in the tree nearby, chained so that it could not be dislodged. The men had slit its stomach to release gastric juices to leave a tempting trail for a predator which would follow to where the donkey had been dragged behind the bush vehicle.

The smell of rumen wafted in the breeze and already the jackals were skipping forward then back from the base of the tree, eyes flashing as they took in the sight of the feast above. The men had, after positioning the donkey, moved into the blind that had been prepared and from there, at intervals, they played the lion-luring sounds over a speaker — taped sounds of hyaena and jackal feeding.

Before these sounds were played, two kilometres away, a large young male lion was resting uneasily beneath a shepherds tree. This was new land Batian had moved into. He had crossed the dry riverbed into South Africa only a few days earlier and was attempting to join up with a group of lionesses. These lionesses had heard feasting sounds beyond the riverbed one night and had hastened towards the sounds. Batian had followed their passage by scent. One of the lionesses he sought was already dead, fooled by the men and taped feeding sounds.

North was Batian's home, the Botswana Tuli bushlands. Here in the south, though eager to join up with the lionesses, Batian's senses were acute with unease and wariness — he did not know this land. Beneath the shepherds tree, he suddenly raised his head, the feeding sounds had reached him. He shifted in one movement into a sitting position and stared with his amber eyes into the sky seeking vultures whose spiral glides signal a death, a kill. Strangely, there were no vultures — sounds of feeding, but no vultures. How was he ever to know what was happening? Men were manipulating his reactions, creating an illusion to lure him to them.

Batian stood, shook his great head to rid himself of the ever-present mopane flies and began to walk in the direction of the feeding sounds.

My lion was recognisable from other males his age because he had only a sad stump of a tail. This and other now healed injuries were sustained in a fight he had fought against two other males. He had nearly died and I had nursed him, staying beside him for three days and nights. A vet then operated upon his severed tail and over the following few weeks, it was his courageous spirit which had enabled him to survive and heal.

As he walked, the sun went down behind the tall sandstone ridge in the west. Then the pungent smell of gastric juices reached him and his nostrils flared. He had reached where the men had dragged the donkey — the lure, the lion bait. Batian lowered his head, sniffing the ground, identifying the direction in which the donkey had been dragged — and then he followed the trail.

After he had continued for some distance, the smell suddenly intensified. Batian stopped and stared around him.

He saw a clearing ahead and gingerly, tempted by the smell, moved forward again. He stopped again upon seeing the donkey trussed up in the tree. In the near distance, he saw too a vehicle. He became increasingly uneasy, equating vehicles with man and that with disturbance. Although he had been reared by man — George Adamson and his staff and rehabilitated into the wilds eventually by myself — he was a wild lion now; an orphan who, with his sisters, had successfully reverted to self-dependence, relying upon now polished instincts and his kind's intelligence.

Batian warily approached the tree and the bait. He was hungry. Then he spun around, hearing an unnatural sound. Whether it was the men's low voices, a movement from within the blind or the loading of rifles, I will never know. Batian faced the hide, then circled to one side, and then perhaps the smell of man touched his senses.

One of the men aimed his rifle, then shot my Batian through his brain. Seconds later, another man shouldered his rifle at Batian's slumped bleeding

6

body and fired the second shot into his ruined head. 'Bastards!' my mind screams as I write these words. 'Bastards!' The four men who had arranged, awaited and carried out the execution of my lion were a game ranch owner, his manager, a professional hunter and his American 'client'. Although it has never been proven, it is possible that in fact Batian was shot for money. This would explain the presence of the professional hunter and his American client. The following day, the ranch owner and his manager were charged with illegally shooting Batian.

For Julie and me, Batian's death marked the dawn of darkness on our lives as we struggled to protect the Tuli lions and the bushlands themselves in the long months ahead.

Just as I was preparing to write this book, three years after Batian's death, I learnt that another young male lion had been shot on the same game ranch — another young male sought and slain. The killers had struck again. As I was about to write about Batian's death, this recent killing echoed the past

7

and resurrected my anger. This killing, however, makes me ever more determined to write of the life of the Adamson lions and life in the Tuli bushlands after Batian's murder — for the lions, for the bushlands . . .

I looked into the recent killing with the help of conservation authorities and a journalist. The journalist telephoned the ranch manager to ask about the killing. The man reacted angrily, asking whether I was behind the questions. He told the journalist to tell me that if it was ever definitely established that an Adamson lion was on his land, he would go out of his way to make sure it died. This man's anger stems from the fact that after Batian's death, he and the ranch owner were found guilty as criminals, fined and sentenced for what they had done.

The journalist repeated his words to me and upon hearing them, I thought, as I have many times during the past three years, 'What would this man's response or action be to me if fate brought us together one day? What would be my own?' To both, perhaps, the only answer for now is a question mark.

1

Killers with a Conscience

BATIAN'S death touched so many people. Children and adults from all over southern Africa and beyond wrote to Julie and me to express their condolences and heartfelt sympathy. He was loved by people of all backgrounds and race. Almost none of the people saw him in real life, only in pictures, and none knew him as we did, but their love for him was abundant. One man wrote, 'Gareth, when you go to rest by the cairn of stones built in memory of Batian, will you please place a stone on it for me?' From the Tuli Safari Area, the neighbouring reserve to us in Zimbabwe, a land where Batian had roamed with a Tuli lioness whom he had mated, warden David Mupungu wrote, 'Gareth, it is indeed most disheartening to learn that Batian has been brutally forced to part company with you in particular,

and every nature-loving person in general
. . . The action taken against Batian is
condemnable, especially when one thinks
of the history behind the Adamson lions.'
Another person wrote, 'When you care
and love a lot, you will have to grieve
a lot, but don't be discouraged as many
of us need the reassurance that there are
people like you prepared to put dreams
into reality and accept both the joy and
sorrow involved.'

I was startled when a psychic medium
friend of mine wrote, 'I have known a
long time of Batian's impending death
. . . I knew it when writing my last letter
to you . . . you will see the clue I planted
in the last paragraph, hinting at the
purpose of his impending death — that
man, who denounces and destroys the
predators is without the nobility and
purity of soul of the animal predators,
and with his greed, he destroys the
world.'

Children have untarnished thoughts
and wisdom. A child wrote, 'When I
heard about Batian, I felt tears run down
my cheeks. But after a month, I realised
that at least he had a chance of Freedom

and you gave it to him. He would have preferred to die young in the wild than to die old in a zoo.'

The cards and poems sent to us made me truly realise what Batian had given to people in the spiritual sense before his death and after. There is a great significance in this, I believe. Why did people react as they did to Batian's death? Is it not in part because in our history, lions are more than animals? From ancient times to today, lions are symbols of courage, power and more. Man draws for himself from the natural world what he sees as admirable and does so with the lion. 'They have impressed themselves so deeply on the human mind, if not its blood, it is as though the psyche were emblazoned with their crest', so wrote Evelyn Ames.[1] George Adamson believed the lion's code of behaviour is worthy of our respect and 'indeed some of their genetic commandments look no worse than ours and are more

---

[1] Ames, Evelyn: *A Glimpse of Eden*, Collins, 1968

11

often heeded. Self-reliance and courage, tenacious yet realistic defence of the realm, the willingness to care for the young or another, brotherhood, loyalty and affection are seven commendable precepts.'

Of the Born Free era, Batian was one of the last of the 'Free'. The first of the 'free' was the lioness, Elsa, and her story wielded tremendous influence on people. With it, there was a rebirth of environmental awareness, her story contributing to the birth of the Green Movement. The spreading Born Free philosophy has reawakened natural customs, such as the importance of kindness and sympathetic understanding to all life. These customs counter the notion of human ascendancy, a myth that has enabled us to live by self-deception, a self-deception that has governed our exploitive behaviour of animals and Nature. It is this same self-deception that gave legitimisation to the ill-treatment by humans of other humans of different race. For example, it is not coincidental that the British abolition of the slave trade in 1807 closely coincided with the earliest Parliamentary debates on cruelty to animals.

It is undeniable that man's historical link with lions has had its influences on man. Today, the symbolism of the Born Free lions is enabling man to question the notion of 'ascendancy' and promotes empathy with other life. The quicker this evolves, the sooner we will check the threats to our own survival. This is the significance, I feel, of the stories of the lives of Elsa . . . and Batian, and others to come. The picture of man and the potent archetype, the lion, together in harmony is full of strong symbolism as it stirs emotions in man's heart that it is natural to identify with and to feel remorse about harming other life. It stirs within us, as we look around at our destruction of this earth, the realisation that we are killers — killers with a conscience.

★ ★ ★

'We are crying for the lions' was my friend, game guide David Marupane's reaction to what had happened to Batian,

13

and the other lions lost. His profession of guiding nature lovers through the bushlands centred greatly upon the lives of the Tuli lion prides, and the individual lions which he and the other guides had come to know so well over the years.

'We are crying for the lions', he exclaimed when we met each other one day while driving upon a road running parallel with the Limpopo river beyond which Batian and others had lost their lives. I asked David which lions he was now seeing on game drives. He replied that he was seeing virtually none apart from Furaha or Rafiki occasionally.

At the beginning of that very year, 1991, Julie and I estimated that the Tuli lion population in the Botswana bushlands had risen to the new height in recent years of about forty-three — of which we estimated forty per cent were cubs. We felt then that our efforts were paying off with the greater protection provided by our anti-poaching team and other initiatives taking place in the area. At last it had seemed the lions were finding their own natural levels. The recent punishing killings

14

were emphasising, however, in the worst possible way, how fragile and sensitive the Tuli lion population was to human impact — an isolated island population where, because of the moat of man surrounding it, no fresh lion immigration or interchange can exist.

It was a most terrible time and despite trying so hard after Batian's death to prevent other lions being shot, the complicated combination of bureaucracy, politics and people's self-interest left us helpless. The exact number of lions killed in the Northern Transvaal will never be known. Of the group of two lionesses and six cubs which Batian had followed into South Africa, only one female and a single cub were seen back in the bushlands. Tragically, the lioness returned with a gunshot wound. Julie and I searched for this lioness and the little one, but never found her. She was seen by game guides upon an impala kill, however, and it was remarkable that she could still kill for herself. We were advised by a veterinary friend not to dart her and operate on her gunshot wound as he felt this could further endanger her.

If she was moving freely and killing, it meant she had a fair chance of survival. In the weeks ahead, though, after several more reported sightings, she and the little one were not seen again, their combined fate unknown to this day.

Some of the lions lured into the Northern Transvaal escaped death and found relative safety on the De Beers Venetia reserve bordering the game ranches. But as they never returned to the bushlands, their loss had a great impact upon the dynamics of the Tuli lion structure.

That year was to be extreme in lion losses, aside from those lost in the Northern Transvaal. On the bushlands un-lion-proofed western boundary, which bordered with livestock farming, a male was killed, as were a lioness and her two cubs (I later saw their skins 'decorating' the walls of what was then the homestead of a cattle concern) and two other lionesses were reported to have been shot. Within the bushlands, the grisly remains of a young male were found near the extreme north-west boundary. His death was thought to have been prolonged after sustaining either a gin trap (see picture section) or bullet injury to the leg. Additionally, this was the year the legendary old male, Darky, disappeared. Monarch of the Lower Majale pride for over a decade, his disappearance was shrouded in mystery.

* * *

Occasionally, Julie and I would drive to the small town of Messina in South Africa to buy vehicle spares and supplies. On the road to this town, one has to drive past the entrance to the ranch on which Batian was killed. The first time we drove past that ranch after his death, we both felt physically sick. After the trip, we returned to the Botswana borderpost of Pont Drift and drove back to camp subdued.

The past few weeks had been an emotional nightmare and we still could not really believe that Batian was gone. Like most days then, when driving back to camp, I would still habitually search for his tracks on the familiar game trails he had so often used. I would sometimes mentally catch myself doing this and would try to snap out of the habit. Just after his death, it was strange and emotionally cruel to see old spoor of his imprinted on the soft ground or in the dry riverbeds. Batian was such a major part of our lives that we would sometimes half convince ourselves that he was not in fact the lion shot and that he would suddenly just appear at the camp, happy, big-hearted and gentle as ever. The wind would slowly erase the last of his paw prints, but the memory of him physically, a golden young prince, remained indelible. All around us were sights and sounds of association — his jetting tree, his favourite lying-up areas, and at night, I would awake to the occasional distant roars of other lions north, thinking it was him. And then the clouds of reality would descend.

At that time, Julie and I would discuss how Furaha and Rafiki would eventually react at some point to his disappearance — would they realise one day that he would not be coming back to them? Initially, it seemed when they visited camp that they thought he was on one

18

of his sojourns north with 'his' lioness. The lionesses would arrive, utter that questioning 'where are you?' call, await a reply for a short moment before sniffing at his jetting tree and at the waterbowls before drinking. Then they would enthusiastically greet me before going off again into the wild country which was theirs, returning to their respective sets of cubs.

On the day we returned from Messina, we discovered Rafiki near the camp and what was to occur later lifted my sombre mood. After driving into camp, I slipped through the gate to call her. Julie watched as Rafiki ran up to me at speed, then leapt up on to her hind legs and with her paws clasped me around the shoulders, and we embraced. After a few seconds, she dropped to all fours and a tremendous greeting continued with her moaning, our headrubbing and my affectionate words. After which, I followed her to where she drank water, and we sat together in the calm of the late afternoon. As I sat beside her, I wondered what she was thinking, her eyes at rest mere slits, but her unsleeping ears reacting to the varied sounds in the bush around as I saw Julie watching us from inside the camp and I wondered what she too was thinking.

When the sun was low, Rafiki began to yawn and then clean her paws, licking them before rubbing them across her face. After which she rose, threw her body against my legs, then walked away. I followed. She and I went at first down the riverbed towards Batian's grave. Her paws and my feet made crunching noises as we stepped on the grey gravelly basalt riverbed. We crossed the riverbed further down and walked another 100 metres east before she made her cub call — the throaty sound she would use to tell the cubs she was near and approaching. At that point, I stopped and watched, expecting her to go into thicker bush where the cubs might be hidden. I was therefore extremely surprised to see her lie down in a clearing next to an old aardvark burrow. She lay there and suddenly — I could not believe my eyes — I saw a cub's head, then another, appear out of the ground at the entrance of the hole. Then all three cubs clambered out excitedly to greet their mother. I watched this magical sight, hidden from the cubs' view. A little later, I stepped quietly away, smiling, and headed to Batian's grave where I stayed for a short while before returning in the twilight to the camp and to Julie.

What I had seen, with Rafiki hiding the cubs in an aardvark burrow, was new lion behaviour to me, behaviour I have not ever seen documented in the literature on lions. Lionesses generally hide their cubs in thick bush, hollows in tall grassy areas etc. — not as I had seen in a hole in the ground in a clearing.

The following day, a sight jolted me directly to thoughts of Batian and further — to questions such as how the death of Batian and the disappearance of the old monarch of the south, Darky, would affect my pride and what remained of that pride in the south. The sight was of one of the last Lower Majale lionesses, way out of her territory in the centre of my pride's area, sitting in some shade where so often I would come across Batian and his sisters. The lioness was lying up by the perennial pool in the Pitsani river, gazing out all around her as if expectant. I knew this Lower Majale lioness well. She was no longer young and was identifiable by a large lump upon her thick neck.

Looking at her, I suspected she was in oestrus and was seeking Batian. Her litter of cubs was now approaching two years old and she left them south as her body told her she could now breed again. She sat there for the entire day, and would occasionally call softly. To me, all around her seemed empty, hollow. Batian's absence was everywhere. It was a strange experience, like knowing a beautiful landscape intimately but one day, when gazing across it, discovering the scene's heart — a spectacular range of hills — is no longer there, and the picture, the scene is incomplete for ever.

As I watched her, I wondered whether Zimmale and his brother, who sired Furaha and Rafiki's cubs, would move south into two separate prides' ranges, prides now without the security of pride males. Would they, I wondered, pose a threat to my lionesses' cubs? Infanticide is common in lion society with the ousting, or death, of a former pride male. New males instinctively kill the past master's cubs, after which the pride lionesses will come into oestrus again. Would Zimmale or his brother kill the cubs, or know that they were their own? I thought about such complex questions as I watched the lioness upon the Pitsani river bank, questions that would only be answered with time.

The first time Julie and I suspected that Furaha and Rafiki realised Batian's loss was one evening when both his sisters appeared together outside the camp. I went out and sat between them. Missing Batian, I almost unconsciously began calling softly the lion proclamation, 'Oowhey, oowhey, oowhey'. Immediately, both lionesses looked up at me with staring open faces. Julie, who was watching, wrote later, 'It was as though they thought of Batian — both became attentive to him. It was a strange scene to watch. Gareth is their pride male now.'

A few days later, Julie was again to witness a strange scene. In the early evening, I heard both lionesses calling softly in the near distance and I went out of the gate to await their arrival at camp. They appeared to greet me, both very jealous of my attention. Then they looked at Julie standing nearby behind the camp fence. I noticed strangely that they then both began staring to a point to the left of her. They remained still, staring. Julie and I looked at each other and then we too looked at the focus of their stares. We could see nothing, just the vehicle track and the wall of our mess hut. Instinctively, Julie's and my eyes met again while still the lionesses' eyes were fixed — not in great curiosity or tense as when they hunt, but with open-faced stares as if seeing something neutral and familiar, not foe or prey. They were seeing what our sense could not, but Julie and I thought the same thing. Then slowly, this time not as intensely and as if preoccupied, they resumed greeting me, but occasionally they would turn back to stare at what was a mysterious presence.

Three weeks later, I witnessed again one of my lionesses reacting to the mysterious presence. I had been following the spoor of a lioness and three cubs (I was not certain whether it was Furaha or Rafiki) up the Pitsani Valley. I saw where the lioness had led her cubs to an aardvark hole, into which the little ones had entered. The lioness's spoor led on and up a tributary stream of the Pitsani. I followed the spoor quietly. After about a kilometre, in quite thick mopane scrub, I saw a lioness resting alone upon the banks of the stream bed. Her head was to one side, her cheek resting upon her paws. She was so much a part of the wilderness canvas, and yet I felt a strange sense of sadness — she seemed at the same time to be so alone. I called softly to her and she looked around her, then without any initial surprise looked at me. It was Furaha and she came forward to greet me, but only for a short while before pushing past me to investigate a few short yards from where I had come. I saw as she then stopped with that same fixed stare on her face which lasted for about five or so seconds. She slowly turned to look at me and returned to me. Once again, the presence of another was felt by us both. I later left Furaha. I walked away with a numbness within me that was strangely comforting.

It was not long after Batian's death that a human tragedy occurred in the Tuli bushlands. Game reserve staff member, Andries Engelbrecht was killed by a bull elephant when returning to his camp on foot after a visit to a trading store. Andries was one of the Tuli's true bush characters and his death came as a great shock to many of us in the bushlands. Andries was an Afrikaans-speaking man who had moved into the area from South Africa many years previously. He married a Tswana lady and worked for some time in the cattle country adjacent to the bushlands before later working in one of the reserves. It was in the cattle country where we had first met and worked together, attempting to relocate Tuli lions under threat of being destroyed for killing livestock.

Deaths by elephant are not uncommon in the bushlands. At the time of Andries' death, three other people were known to have been killed in the last two years. I say 'known' as I suspect others had died, but that their deaths went undiscovered. This is because every year literally hundreds of Zimbabweans cross the bushlands illegally at night to seek work on the neighbouring South African farmlands. Stumbling into an elephant herd in the thick riverine bush of the Shashe and Limpopo rivers is a real danger for these Zimbabweans, an awful risk they have to take in order to seek employment and earn a livelihood.

However, Andries' death was probably a freak accident. He knew elephants and their behaviour well. He was a skilled bush man, but like all of us who live in the wilds, the odds of an accident mount increasingly the more time one spends there, no matter how cautious one is. These odds are simply a fact of life. The risk of death by wild animals for the Zimbabweans is far greater, however, simply because of the sheer numbers walking each year in the dark of night through the bushlands.

In the early 1980s, I remember witnessing the aftermath of an elephant attack on a Zimbabwean which had occurred at night. At the time, I was working in a camp on the banks of the

27

Limpopo adjacent to South Africa. One morning, I heard urgent shouts from across the river and, with my tracker, I investigated. A man shouted across to us that his father lay dead several kilometres from where we stood. He had walked into an elephant herd the night before. We then drove to where it was thought the tragedy had occurred. We reached the approximate area, then drove slowly off the road. The trackers and I were tense and extremely watchful for signs of elephants. As we turned into a small clearing, we were startled by the damage around us — the bush and the trees were torn and broken. It was as if an elephant herd had been in a mad frenzy of destruction. Then amidst the smashed bush and trampled ground, we saw an old man standing quiet and still next to a large tree. We approached and the trackers spoke to him in low calming tones. He was clearly in shock, but otherwise unharmed and after a while, he led us to where his companion lay dead. It was my first experience of seeing a dead person. I saw a man lying face down on the ground, his broken limbs at crooked, abnormal angles. My initial reaction was a sense of unreality. He lay there as though asleep, but all life had left him. I saw too where a tusk had entered the middle of his back.

The old Zimbabwean told us that the night before, he and his companion had walked unknowingly into a large herd of elephants — although it may seem unbelievable, a herd of elephants can be incredibly quiet at times. Both men had fled, but only he had escaped. The elephants, he told us, had screamed and trumpeted in their fear and anger, smashing the bush before running away to the north and away from the scene. It was a chilling reminder to me, then a young game ranger, of just one of the many faces death has in the wilds.

The Tuli elephants, due to their past history of persecution by man, are aggressive at times. Many of the old Tuli elephants would have witnessed the government's culling of their family members thirty years previously in a large area north-west of the reserves — a wide tract of their former range in which over a thousand elephants died to make way for people and settlement. At the time of that killing, it was discovered that some sixty per cent of those that died had either old or fresh gunshot wounds. Today, when Tuli elephants kill man, it is not due to any evil malice, but as a result of fear and protection of their young.

During the course of my work, I spent thousands of hours either with the lions or undertaking anti-poaching patrols. No one was spending as much time on foot in the bushlands as I was. It was good fortune, as well as my constant vigilance, that although potentially close calls occurred, I always managed to avoid a life-threatening incident with Tuli elephants. Julie would say sometimes that I must have a guardian angel looking after me. I was, in view of the odds, incredibly lucky, particularly as for a substantial part of the time then and in the months ahead, I had no firearm.

Hearing of Andries' death, I was saddened and was reminded again of the times we had worked together trying desperately to save the cattle-killing lions. To highlight the problem at that time, the following is what I wrote in a report to prompt action for the lions' protection:

On 5 February, as the shots rang out, the heavily pregnant lioness slumped to the ground, blood soaking into her golden coat at the shoulder and hindquarters. Confused by the noise, the remaining lions moved swiftly into the gloom of the undergrowth, hidden also by the gathering twilight, to where luckily they could no longer be followed. I was shown the body the following morning. The gruesome sight of the skinned lioness pained me considerably as there, in the dirt, reduced from her majesty, she lay — a broken body of raw flesh. The dead lioness was the mother of a young male who had reached sub-adulthood. As he was now approaching two years old, the lioness had mated with the pride male and conceived again. Inside her bloated body were found two cubs which, if the lioness had not been shot, would have been born within a month.

The slaughter of the lions in the cattle country the year of Batian's death was yet another example of a perennial problem not being addressed at that time by the owners of the reserves. For years, lions have been attracted by the scent and sight of cattle beyond the western boundary and they go and kill the easy prey. What would reduce the loss of cattle and save lion life is the electrification of wire strands placed low on the existing fence. In my experience, Tuli lions crawl under fences as opposed to climbing over them to venture into the cattle country. But as no lion deterrent strands exist on the fences, lions have been lost every year and in addition, there have been cattle losses, which understandably evoke hostility from the local people.

Andries and I spent time together in 1985 cautiously tracking a particular cattle-killing pride which normally resided in the reserve. They were moving out increasingly due to the superabundance of livestock. We would locate the lions on foot, following spoor, then lure them with a bait to where at night a darting and relocating exercise would be attempted.

Most cold winter nights, we would fail as this pride was shy and suspicious of man. One night, though, the pride grew more confident, at last becoming more conditioned to the vehicles and our presence. At 3.30 in the morning, our vet, Andrew, managed to dart a young male, but the rest of the pride fled. Soon we were driving a peacefully sedated young male back to the core of the pride's range in the reserve — but we had great doubts as to whether our efforts would achieve anything. We felt that the youngster would, upon waking, trek back to the rest of the pride in the cattle country. This he duly did the following night.

One night, when I did not accompany the darting team, Andrew managed to dart a young female. He decided to keep her captive while we attempted to dart other pride members, then to release them altogether as a group in the core area. He felt this method might encourage the lions to remain in the centre of their territory. It was at this point that our earnest work took a humorous twist that was also a knife edge away from being potentially tragic.

After darting and loading the lioness, Andrew was in a dilemma as to where to contain her until her release, hopefully with other pride members, the following day. No lion enclosure existed in the reserve and Andrew, in desperation, decided to put the lioness in a sturdy store room at his camp. This he did, leaving her peacefully still sedated.

That night, Andrew and I had another cold and frustrating wait. The lions had become wary again and no darting took place. As the sun's rays began to filter through on the horizon, we, tired and chilled to the bone, decided to return to his camp. Upon reaching it, we felt that we should not keep the lioness (now fully conscious) in the store room any longer.

Unfortunately, the store room door only opened inwardly, thus making her release somewhat difficult. Andrew decided to climb up on to the store room's flat roof and manipulate the door open with a pole. This he successfully managed. I remained near another building with the trackers, holding my rifle ready to let off a warning shot should the lioness come out to regard Andrew angrily on top of the roof. As the door opened, we expected her to bound out to freedom. Instead, there was not a movement from within. Andrew shrugged his shoulders before beginning to bang on the roof in an attempt to scare her out. Again, there was no movement. The suspense grew. Still on the roof, Andrew decided to shoot a dart (without a needle) at her rump. Through a small window, he pointed his dart gun and fired. Unbelievably the situation remained the same.

It was at this point that I called to Andrew suggesting that I pass a nearby hosepipe up to him so he could spray water at the lioness through the same small window. Andrew agreed, but said he would fetch the hosepipe himself. He climbed off the roof and I stared anxiously at the open store room door. The tap and pipe were some fifty metres away and upon reaching them, he turned on the tap and picked up the hose. As the water began to spill out and as he was about to return to the store room, suddenly

I saw a tawny flash. The lioness was dashing from the store, heading directly for Andrew. I leapt forward, yelling at the lioness at the top of my voice. This all happened in an instant. She reacted to my shouts, turned and fled, stumbling once before disappearing into the bush. I was now standing close to Andrew, and he was staring at where she had gone. I then turned to Andrew. I will always remember the picture of him still holding the hosepipe from which water poured, the ground soaked around his feet. His face was ashen. We collectively let out a huge sigh of relief and began laughing idiotically.

Unfortunately that and many other of our darting operations proved to be futile. The lions, once darted and moved back into the reserve, always eventually returned to the cattle country where many were to die. In 1986, I concluded: 'It was a frustrating and hopeless situation . . . Until the (electric) fence was erected and for many other reasons, there was nothing more I could do to protect the lions and in the months to come, their numbers tragically declined, one by one.'

Sadly, today in 1995, predator-deterrent fencing still does not exist, and cattle killing continues as does the killing of lions. The killing is on a reduced scale, but ironically this is because there are so few lions left to leave the reserve to prey upon livestock. It is a sad, sad situation, one which could have been rectified a long time ago if only the need for the greater protection of Tuli lions had been admitted and made a priority by the Tuli reserve owners.

2

A Chapter of Conflict

THE year 1991 was indeed emotionally bruising for Julie and me in the bushlands. Much of this centred on Batian's death, but as well as that tragedy, we faced other major problems and we also faced criticism. For example, earlier in the year, the Landowners' Association imposed rigid censorship rules and regulations upon us. This was in reaction to a report I had compiled which reviewed our work and shared ideas for much-needed initiatives in the bushlands. I had sent the report to both the association and the Department of Wildlife. The report's contents were written honestly and, I felt, objectively, and never did I imagine that the association would react to it in the way that it did. If I had, I obviously would not have written it and sent it to them.

The rules included a clause stating that anything I wished to publish or write about the bushlands in the future had first to be cleared by the landowners' committee. This also included the contents of any interview that I intended to give. I was told that if they considered it 'detrimental to the reserve, it will be vetoed'. Additionally, I was informed that Julie and I were to have no communication with the Botswana government except through them, or otherwise only with their authority. I was told that my writing on the Tuli lion population, of its vulnerability and the damaging impact upon it of poaching was 'in the negative and creates a general impression of doom and disaster for the Tuli'. Julie was additionally criticised for what she had written in a magazine article. In the article, she had truthfully stated 'his [my] findings led him to write his first book, *Cry for the Lions* — the story of the demise of the Tuli lions'. The committee claimed somehow that this totally misrepresented the position in the Tuli, and would discourage tourism. I would agree with the last statement, but only in another sense. Yes, the demise of the Tuli lions was detrimental to tourism because tourists were seeing fewer lions. They also felt it was their prerogative as owners to decide what could be published about the reserve and what could not, and that even if our writings were deemed valid that they reserved the right to veto publication of such material.

These rulings were tied into the lease agreement allowing us to remain at our camp until the following April. When that lease lapsed, of course, we would not be subject to the rulings, but we would also be without a field base. Being censored frustrated us greatly as we lived amidst issues that were not being addressed. Although Julie and I continued to do what we as individuals could for the bushlands, ultimately, unless the landowners were steered towards constructively conserving the area as a whole, or until government put greater emphasis on an obligation to the owners to protect this particular portion of the country's natural heritage, we were fighting an uphill battle.

None of my writings were, of course, intended to be detrimental to the area.

Our cause was after all the bushlands. It was the bushlands and its animal inhabitants to which we were dedicated. No one paid us to undertake our conservation work on this privately owned land and we financed what we did mostly from our own limited resources.

When people ask why such rules and regulations were placed on us and our work, I cannot give a completely clear answer. I feel, however, that the answer centres upon what can be described as traditional 'white fears' — the landowners' insecurity in relation to the future ownership of these lands. The majority of the reserves were owned by absentee white South Africans — many portions of which were used purely for the owners' exclusive recreation, were non-revenue earning and the owners' livelihoods were not dependent upon their land. In the 1980s, the Botswana parliament, due to the lack of a common adoption of a Conservation Strategy by the landowners, considered the acquisition of these Tuli reserves for the formation of a National Game Reserve. Unfortunately, this did not occur but nevertheless the spectre of nationalisation hung over the landowners' heads and still does.

In a short history of the Landowners' Association, compiled by one of the oldest members, the following was written when summing up the situation in 1991: 'Threat of nationalisation of all farms in the area is still very real. The whole bushveld atmosphere is not what it used to be when the true hunting sportsmen cared for and protected their game. Poaching is now back in full swing.' And when contemplating the future, he wrote 'completely unpredictable'.

So the voice of our conservation watchdog presence for the bushlands was now temporarily silenced during the following six-month lease period so we could remain at our Tawana Camp.

That year, we faced criticism from yet another quarter, this time on scientific grounds. In a letter to the editor, published in a prominent South African wildlife magazine, a member of the IUCN's Cat Specialist Group, Professor Helmut Hemmer of the Johannes Gutenberg University in Germany, strongly criticised my work with the lions. The letter was entitled 'A contribution to conservation?'. He was opposing my work on the grounds of genetics, the mixing of Kenyan and Botswanan lions in the bushlands. This letter sparked controversy and a row. It advocated that my lions be neutered while expressing comment on what he perceived as being the possible detrimental genetic consequences of the project. The issue was genetic purity and he felt my lions could not only affect the resident Tuli lion population, but might be a future source of remodelling the genetic make-up of other Botswanan lion populations. To me, this conjured up thoughts of the past where an Aryan race was advocated.

In further published letters, I was criticised by the chairman of the Cat Specialist Group, Peter Jackson. He wrote, I feel rather rashly, 'Neither Adamson nor Patterson's work with lions is a contribution to lion conservation . . . they create a misleading conception of conservation problems and remedies and divert funds which could be better used for the real thing.' These comments irritated me then, I feel that he probably regrets writing them today. By criticising George, he automatically offended legions of the public worldwide who drew environmental awareness, 'green' concern and spiritual inspiration from the Born Free legend. In contrast to Jackson's criticism, George Schaller, perhaps the greatest authority on the behaviour of carnivores and who pioneered the study of the lion in the Serengeti, wrote this recently of George's (and Joy's) contribution: 'Their effort at reintroduction and rehabilitation taught the scientific community invaluable lessons and the conservation community will be forever indebted to them. The Adamsons gave us truths about the species that cannot be found in a biologist's note book.'

As for the diverting of funds, George battled financially for years and what did Jackson know of the funding of my project? We did not exist on public monies, at the time receiving only occasional donations from friends and supporters. Without my limited book royalties and Julie draining her savings, we could not have continued after the initial sponsorship ran out. We struggled to raise money and legally were unable to solicit donations in South Africa as we were not granted a fundraising number. Lions are 'not seen as endangered', we had been told.

Jackson, like Hemmer, recommended that my lions be neutered and 'if cubs are born as a result of the reported mating, they too will have to be dealt with'. I remember these words as I sat in the heart of the bushlands watching Rafiki attending to her cubs in her nursery hideout not twenty yards away. His statements were loftily made and appeared to lack a drop of compassion for these, my lions — individuals of a species. Without compassion, I asked myself, what is the motivation for what we do to help other life? Was Jackson in reality on a mission against what he perceived or was conditioned to perceive as 'sentimentality'?

I replied to the original letter of criticism, but when it was published in the magazine, italicised comments by two professional conservationists were inserted between my main points which interrupted the flow of my letter. It also cast doubts in my mind as to the objectivity of this magazine's editorial policy. Some of the italicised comments were spiteful and patronising such as, 'or does the public prefer the George Adamson/Gareth Patterson razzmatazz and Tarzan syndrome?' when commenting upon George's and my work.

An article in the BBC *Wildlife* magazine was headed, 'Foreign Lion Genes terrorise Scientists'. The gene issue did upset some scientists, but interestingly, it transpired that members of the Cat Specialist Group were themselves divided on the issue. There was Hemmer on one side with his concern for purity of lion genetics, while world-renowned cat specialist, Dr Paul Leyhausen argued that the difference between my lions and Tuli lions could only be 'a matter of statistically different allele distribution. Any alleles — or modified gene — which didn't fit would quickly be bred out.' In India, famous tiger specialist and author, Billy Arjan Singh, opposed Hemmer's comments that my project was 'a clear anti-conservation act'. In Singh's view, he felt that this remark 'illustrates narrow scientific dogma, which seeks to override rational conservation measures. In these days of rapidly changing values, science should subserve the aims of conservation and not vice versa.' I endorsed this.

Members of the public wrote supportive letters to Julie and me. The writer of the following was reacting to the italicised comments mentioned earlier.

I was disgusted by the uncouth and disgracefully rude remarks in the magazine letter section. If it were not for people like you and George Adamson, little would be known about lions by the general public . . . I don't always care for the tone of the articles . . . (in that magazine) . . . in which compassion towards animals is often missing.

I began to prepare a similar lengthy letter of reply to the criticism levelled by sectors of the Cat Specialist Group. I pointed out factors that should have been taken into consideration before the attacks were made upon George's work and mine. One aspect I stressed was that the Tuli bushlands is a wilderness surrounded by man and that, because of this island scenario, sadly no immigration of lions from other areas can occur which, under circumstances unaffected by man, would have taken place and would have maintained genetic diversity of the Tuli lion population. Additionally, I emphasised that the demise of the lions in the bushlands by brutal persecution in the 1950s had created a bottleneck situation and the decline of lions that I had recorded in the past, together with the present decline, the result of the recent killings, would have had damaging implications in relation to genetic diversity and that the population could hardly be termed 'healthy'.

Although not a scientist, I was of the view that by introducing my lions in to the bushlands, it was inevitable that diversification of the limited gene pool would occur. I also stated that it must be remembered that the lion population of East and Southern Africa was historically largely interjoining and that it was only due to the comparatively recent impact of man that this situation no longer existed, and this is why small restricted populations have resulted, of which the Tuli is a classic example.

Even though at the time the controversy was unpleasant, it nevertheless offered the opportunity then and now of focusing emphasis on the decrease and fragmentation of the African lion's range and what the implications were of this when coupled with close inbreeding. The question I asked then and ask again now is, yes, lions may occur in hosts of African game reserves, but of those reserves, how many contain a population of several hundred which would maintain that the population is in fact genetically viable? Today, in the whole of South Africa (where lions once roamed from the Cape mountains to the Limpopo), despite lions being introduced in small numbers into other parts of their former range, genetically (long-term) viable populations exist in only two areas — the Kruger National Park and the Kalahari Gemsbok Park adjoining the Botswana Kalahari system.

The well-documented 'island' lion population in Tanzania's Ngorongoro

Crater gives clear indications of the dangers facing fragmented, small, isolated lion populations elsewhere in Africa. The Crater lions may physically look like any other wild lions, but this conceals genetic vulnerabilities of the small population. Close in-breeding of animals can also cause a significant reduction in reproduction and infant survival.

The study by Craig Parker in the Crater first indicated that no new lions had moved into the Ngorongoro during a four-year period. This population in 1962 had been devastated by a plague of biting flies resulting in the number of lions crashing from at least seventy to only ten. Their numbers recovered, but not so the genetic diversity. Parker's study included an analysis of genetics in the Crater lions' blood enzymes and the results suggested extensive in-breeding — an almost unknown phenomenon in the lions of the Serengeti beyond the Crater's walls. The Crater lions' estimated genetic diversity was also much lower than that of their Serengeti counterparts. Semen samples showed high levels of abnormality — a further indication of close in-breeding.

In a second genetic survey, it was revealed that there was an extreme lack of genetic variability in the Crater lions' immune defence systems, leaving these lions incredibly susceptible to a naturally occurring epidemic. Returning to the Tuli, it was dangerous that some of our critics had given the impression that the Tuli lion population was healthy, and close to the number that the area could sustain and that there was immigration of lions occurring from other areas. How I wished this was true. The fact is that there are parallels between the Tuli lions and those of the Ngorongoro Crater (but due to different causes) and how many other such island lion populations are suffering in the same way throughout Africa? This is something that the Cat Specialist Group should act upon.

Protecting such populations from poachers and hunters is not enough — the lion is today in peril, restricted by boundaries imposed by human pressure. The focusing of criticism on my work uncovered an issue that cannot be ignored any longer: the threat of the silent foe, genetic erosion — a symptom of the decrease and fragmentation of the African lion's natural range due to man.

3

Living in Lion Life

I AWOKE on my stretcher, but remained immobile. The low menacing growl reverberated in the night air. I then slowly turned my head towards the camp fence and in the light of a stub of a bravely flickering candle, I saw Zimmale. With my head low, not eighteen inches from the ground, he looked enormous, a spectre of shadows licked with gold as the glow of the light crossed him intermittently. He was just two paces away and stared at me as he rumbled. I stared back, captivated by his presence, half not wanting him there and half not wanting this meeting between us to cease. The experience was a mesmerising one. I was in little danger due to the tall fence dividing us, yet I felt a surge of adrenalin and my blood beat like a drum in my head.

Zimmale turned and slowly sniffed long

53

and probing at Batian's scent-marking bush, then turned to look at me again. Abruptly, the rumbling growls ceased. Then, in a silence that was as eerie as his growls, he stepped back before turning to disappear in the colossal total shadow that was the night.

With Zimmale, a being of the night, entering the flickering glow of my circle of light, I had experienced what our ancestors would have feared most — the appearance of the great hunter of the African darkness, the African night closing in on man, the predatory primate of the daylight. Ancient man had no fence and I felt that if there had been none between us that night, he would have experimentally seized my form. As I was lying horizontally, he perhaps would not have recognised me as human — not a normally preferred prey species of the lion. He might have seized me and mauled me, and upon recognising my kind, would have left me for those of more catholic tastes — the hyaenas, the jackals. I had experienced an encounter that had awoken a part of my ancestral soul and I had felt that soul lift momentarily to a plane higher than this life — as it would have risen permanently if an attack had taken place. I wondered how long he had been looking at me, edging closer until he came up against the fence, as I lay there sleeping.

I remained still, staring south to where he had disappeared. Minutes later, I heard in the distance the sudden alarm snorts of the impala, the rapid sounds that signal that a predator has been sighted, upon which all those around become watchful and alert. Because of these sounds, I knew he was passing through my pride's territory, down the Pitsani to the Lower Majale where there too, with Darky's mysterious disappearance, were the remnants of a pride without a master.

Lying there, I thought of the following words of George Schaller,[1] which perhaps in part reflected what I had experienced: 'Our dual past still haunts us. We hear a lion roar and the primate in us

---

[1] Schaller, George: *Serengeti: A Kingdom of Predators*, Collins.

shivers. We see huge herds of game and the predator in us is delighted, as if our existence still depended on their presence.' With these words and the image of Zimmale still in my mind, I then fell asleep. Despite what I had experienced, I had strangely not been prompted to hurriedly move my stretcher away from the fence and move into my tent. This I feel was an unusual reaction. Despite having the fence between us, the encounter should have unnerved me much more and released the fear of my ancestors — but, as I have written, part of me did not want my meeting with him to cease. It was perhaps because I was so immersed in his kind's world, the world of lion life within which I too lived with my pride, that caused me to react as I did. I was totally alone in the camp that night — the only human for miles around — but I had felt no substantial fear nor the insecurity of aloneness.

When I awoke again hours later at dawn, the candle was a hard white mess melted and moulded on to the earth and I wondered if I had not dreamed of Zimmale. I rose from the stretcher and stepped over to the fence. There I saw his spoor beside the wire and the pugmarks where he had disappeared south. He had been there. It was no dream.

From that night on, my life and those of my pride were about to change. Zimmale perhaps had, before the previous night, sensed Batian was no more. By coming right up to the camp, sniffing for information at Batian's scent-marking tree, he had confirmed his suspicions. His presence in my pride's territory increased steadily from that day, making my pride and me watchful.

I must point out that for the initial four months of Furaha and Rafiki's cubs' lives, both lionesses lived separately, not rejoining as a pride even when the cubs were active and mobile. This was strange and whenever they separately visited me on the same evening, they made no — or only limited — attempts to greet each other as the sisters of blood that they were. For that initial four-month period, their separate litters were their focus and they hunted alone. It was partly these cubs, however, that brought the sisters together again to share comradeship.

At this time, increasingly, the lionesses would bring their cubs with them when visiting me. Julie and I then began witnessing both lionesses and their cubs arriving at the same time but from quite different directions. We would watch as the lionesses remained aloof, but the cubs of the two litters were fascinated by each other. Eventually, once the little ones became familiar to each other, they would become highly excited when meeting outside the camp. They would rush forwards towards each other, calling their 'eeoh . . . eeoh . . . eeoh!' cub call. Despite this, Rafiki and Furaha were initially very possessive of their litters and would even have short sharp conflicts, which was distressing to witness.

We called the litters the 'icebreakers' as inevitably complete reintegration took place with Rafiki and Furaha once again becoming the loving sisters they, beneath their possessiveness, always were. They suckled each other's cubs at times, the two litters became one gambolling, playful group of baby lions, and the lionesses once again began hunting as a competent team, regularly pulling down big prey such as the massive eland. As the cubs, despite still suckling, increasingly needed meat, such large kills were vital — and this is where Zimmale's presence in their range created conflict and stress. He sought to take advantage of these frequent kills and would trail the pride's passage in the bushlands in anticipation of finding them, chasing them away and absconding with the kills.

As the cubs grew, I saw signs that proved that Furaha and Rafiki would not give up a kill without fierce opposition. I suspected on certain occasions that they actually kept Zimmale at bay and successfully defended their kills. One night, I witnessed a clash over a kill between my lionesses and Zimmale with another lioness (which I suspected was his sister). It was early in October and the evening before I discovered that Furaha and Rafiki had ambushed and pulled down an eland cow approximately 800 metres south of Tawana. In the twilight, I spotted my pride resting up, cubs included, near the eland after their initial bout of feeding. So as not to disturb them (the cubs would have scattered upon seeing me unexpectedly), I crept away and returned to camp and told Julie of the scene I had discovered.

Pre-dawn the following morning, I was awoken by the sound of lions fighting, a sound that had haunted me since the time of Batian's near-fatal clash with two other males months before. Julie and I hastily dressed and ran to our vehicle before driving out of camp scanning with the spotlight in my hand. In the south, I suddenly spied Zimmale, large, rangy and loose-bodied, trotting away into thick bush — away from where the eland lay. I feared one of my lionesses might have been injured in a clash with the much larger male. Then I saw he was in fact being driven away as, in the swing of my spotlight, I saw Furaha and Rafiki rushing in long, heavy bounds towards the kill and where he was disappearing. Their appearance caused the hordes of jackals to scatter like cascading marbles from a split bag — their small forms ricocheting away in all directions. I then saw my lionesses rushing back to where I suspected they had left the cubs who undoubtedly would have been scared by the commotion and the appearance of the shaggy-maned Zimmale and his sister.

Then, twice again, like a golden wave, side by side, almost bound by bound, my lionesses rushed to their kill. It was a powerful scene, these two lionesses raised by man were engulfed by the spirit and drive of their wild lion hearts. I was incredibly proud of them. Zimmale's lioness all this time had kept discreetly out of sight.

At sunrise, I returned to the kill site expecting to see my pride in residence. I was surprised, therefore, to discover that Zimmale and the lioness had taken possession. Perhaps hampered by fears for the safety of their cubs, my lionesses had, after their defensive display, deserted the kill and led the young ones away. As I approached, both Zimmale and the lioness began to exhibit menacing behaviour towards me.

I returned later in the day only to discover that they too had strangely deserted the kill. In a few short hours, the eland had been reduced to mere picked bone and hide. The real winners of the feast were the scavengers, like the jackals and particularly the efficient vultures, who now, with bulging gizzards, draped the trees. They balanced unsteadily in the trees all around, some flying off with a mad flapping of wings as they attempted to defy their fullness and gravity as I passed beneath them.

★ ★ ★

Another eland kill, this time of a full-grown bull, occurred even closer to camp just weeks later. One overcast morning, Julie and I heard a strange bellowing and at first thought that elephant were nearby. Not convinced, though, after a while I ventured out of camp to investigate. Minutes later, I came across Furaha and Rafiki walking through the bush followed by their cubs. What I did not know was that they had left their kill (the sounds being the death bellows of the eland), returned to where they had left the cubs and now were leading them to the gargantuan feast. I followed behind, hidden, then spied the body of the immense eland lying in front of where they were headed.

I returned to camp to let the lionesses and cubs feast before going back to the kill site for Julie's and my share. Julie and I used to crave meat and Julie even suffered an iron deficiency, partially due to this lack of meat in her diet. We had no permission to shoot game for our own consumption and meat was prohibitively expensive for us much of the time. On occasions, staff at some of the camps would kindly give us some of their meat 'ration' but otherwise, it was on days like this that the lions would inadvertently supply us with meat. Normally, I would only discover their large kills too late when time and the heat had turned the meat too rank for human consumption — but just right for the lions. My scavenging from them was not the conflict and stressful situation that Zimmale would cause! In fact, on such occasions, they never showed resentment if, after an initial feeding bout, I appeared and cut off some choice portions.

Much later in the day, armed with a specially sharpened knife, I left camp and approached the nearby kill site. The cubs were not to be seen and were probably lying up asleep with full bellies in the nearby thickets. Furaha was, I saw, on her back, white (full) tummy and four legs skywards while Rafiki sat near the carcass, guarding it, with a bloodied face and distended stomach. As I approached, I called to them. Furaha lazily turned her head to look at me, then resumed her half slit-eyed blissful snoozing, while Rafiki wandered up to me and greeted me gently.

With greetings complete, I then walked up to the eland and set about cutting away one of the arm-long 'backstraps' and with this job complete, I cut away several other pieces of meat. Carrying the meat in both hands, I started to head towards camp. As I walked, Rafiki came to my side and, I feel, displaying some mischievousness, began to show much interest in the meat I was carrying despite there being over three-quarters of a ton of eland lying just metres away. I handed her a piece and she playfully skipped to one side, then crouched to feed. I started onwards again when I saw her leave the meat, and come up to me again, expressing interest in the other meat I held. I had to repeat the procedure, handing her another piece but I then returned to reclaim the original piece from the ground. This I did and again attempted to walk away when, once more, Rafiki left the second piece and eyed what I held. I gave her some more and when she took it away, I picked up the second piece and hurried away from the ridiculous situation.

Soon I was a hundred metres away and turning my head, I saw Rafiki had tired of the game and had returned to feed at the eland. My stomach rumbled as I thought of the meat I was carrying for our consumption. Then suddenly, out of the corner of my eye, I saw a lioness speeding towards me. Furaha, who had no doubt been watching Rafiki and me, now decided to join in the proceedings. Fortunately, after she rushed up to me, I managed to fob her off with just a single piece.

I got back to camp with the rest of the meat, including several mangled pieces covered in sand, grass and lion saliva. Julie and I did not complain, however. Soon we were setting about making biltong (dried spiced meat). We cut the meat into long strips, then marinated them before hanging most of it up to dry out. We kept a copious amount for the two of us to fry. That night, Julie and I lay contented with full stomachs on our stretchers, contented like my lions who were near the eland over the rise. Zimmale, on this occasion, disturbed neither party.

The pride fed wholeheartedly on the eland for four days before eventually deserting what remained. Then it was the time of the jackals and vultures whose patience was rewarded. That evening, the hyaenas, with their strong bone-cracking jaws, feasted. Some time during the night, a competing clan appeared and the air thrilled with a shrieking eerie row that awoke us many times that night. The following morning, I returned to the kill site and, yet again, was aghast at how the carcass had been almost totally dismembered, devoured or scattered. Some large bones and the skull and horns of the eland were largely all that remained — the absence of others remains a testimony to the effectiveness of scavengers, large and small. The lions, as always, had provided for a varied host of other life.

After leaving the eland kill, the lions, I discovered, had headed east to the reserve's far eastern boundary — the sand river of the Shashe. In an area of thick bush, permanent water and a high density of traversing game, they remained for over three weeks and there I observed them killing yet another eland right upon the lip of the river bank. My pride's movement out of their traditional core area was influenced heavily by the presence of Zimmale who at this time appeared near Tawana after the eland feast. He then remained in the Pitsani and Tawana valleys, wandering at night in search of my pride. That was until one day he drifted south for a time before eventually residing, until his death, two years later, as pride master of the Shalimpo lions, those lions that lurked in the dense riverine bordering the great sand river of the Shashe.

★ ★ ★

It was November 1991 and the time had now come for me to leave the bushlands and the lions for a two-week period. I flew to what could not be a more contrasting environment to that of my own — to London, England. I was to promote my book *The Lion's Legacy*, which told of my time with George Adamson at Kora. From deep within the lions' world, I found myself in the hubbub and bustle of Britain's capital, but my heart remained with my pride. I was interviewed on national television as well as on radio shows. The actual launch of the book took place at the prestigious Royal Geographical Society in Kensington where I gave a slide presentation on the rehabilitation of my lions and the work of our Tuli Lion Trust. Unfortunately, resources did not allow Julie to accompany me. She remained loyally in the bushlands, based at the Charter Reserve's warden's camp (he was on leave) and in addition to her other work, she monitored the lions as best she could. She occasionally went to Tawana to see whether the lions had visited the camp. She discovered that during the entire fortnight I was away, they did not come to the camp at all as far as she could ascertain.

Julie's mother came from South Africa to stay with her some of the time I was away. Julie had very much wished to introduce her mother to her way of life, to give her an insight into why she was so dedicated to our cause. The weather was extremely hot, they were plagued with punctures and Julie had to cope with a myriad of problems which cropped up at the warden's camp. In turn Julie's mother did, because of the problems, gain a greater insight into Julie's life in the wilds — unfortunately mostly on the downside.

But one afternoon, though, they witnessed an uplifting sight. They were driving in the high northern country when Julie suddenly spotted a lioness, moving in the golden light upon the ridge. She recognised it as Rafiki. It was an important moment because, as she later wrote: 'I was watching a wild lioness out there, on her own, doing her own thing. I think it was the first time I saw "Squeaks" [Rafiki's nickname] as a

lioness, not as a "personality" I knew.'
It has to be remembered that Julie only
normally saw the lions when they visited
camp and was only used to that part of
their lives and not the stalking, killing,
territory-patrolling side I was exposed to
and of which I was a part.

While Julie coped admirably with
keeping the warden's operation running
and supervising the anti-poaching team,
my stress levels fluctuated in Britain.
I rushed from interview to interview,
somewhat claustrophobic and lost in the
bustling crowds, and felt great unease
using the underground subway systems.
Whenever possible, to avoid using public
transport, I walked to appointments. On
one of these walks, I made rather a
fool of myself because of my deepset
bush instincts. I crossed a busy road
and strolled along the busy pavement.
Suddenly, my bush instincts erupted in
the heart of London when I glanced at
something on the ground. I leapt high
and backwards, colliding with several
people. After apologising to what were
already hurriedly departing backs from
which mutters could be heard, I then

looked at the pavement once again. I had mistaken a crack in the concrete for a snake!

On another occasion I was fascinated to see a city person's response when approached by a being with a wild heart in one of London's parks. I was walking through a large park and saw a young lady in the distance stepping briskly and businesslike, briefcase in hand, pads in jacket shoulders, heels clicking on the path. She held her head high and her lips stern. As we approached each other, I suddenly saw a grey squirrel bounce across the lawn and head directly towards the lady as if it had known her for all its life. I watched the lady stop and stare incredulously as the cheerful animal bounded up to her. Then her shoulders dropped, a smile lit up her face and she bent down to the squirrel. As I passed, she had turned to sit on a nearby bench and was pulling out from her briefcase what I presumed was her lunchtime sandwich to share with the little one of a free wild heart in the city of millions of humans. To me, the scene emphasised that whatever the

71

environs, man must be allowed to have contact with what is natural and wild for it is essential for spiritual upliftment and attunement to the natural world. It was a delightful, heartening scene I had witnessed.

★ ★ ★

Soon the book promotion was over and I was flying back to South Africa where I was met by Julie. I was eager to return to learn of the lions' movements and their welfare. Julie had recorded that the pride had resided once again in the rich game country of the Shashe riverbanks and had not once visited our camp in my absence. We had seen before how the lions would somehow know whether I was in the bushlands or not, and would appear outside the camp whenever we returned, on occasions within hours of our arrival after we had been away for days. This was to be the case on my return from Britain. Within a day of our return, knowing that the lions were across at the Shashe, we were flabbergasted when Furaha appeared mysteriously the following morning. Our greetings were excited and this was repeated when that evening both lionesses appeared at dusk, accompanied by their cubs, who kept largely out of sight.

It was a happy homecoming, but as I tried to count all six cubs, I suspected one was missing. Sadly, we confirmed this the next time we saw the pride. One of Furaha's cubs was not with the pride. The cub's disappearance could have been caused by a variety of reasons, such as being inadvertently separated from the rest of the pride, or an attack by another predator, or disease. I felt another possibility was a snakebite, particularly as the cub's disappearance was sudden. The anti-poaching unit had at this time consistently observed spoor of all six cubs when they patrolled and just one day prior to my return from Britain, the spoor of only five cubs had been seen.

It had been wonderful watching the cubs grow and learn recently. I had observed them intently stalking small creatures such as francolin or guineafowl and even at only five months old, they would occasionally participate in the hunt of small herds of impala. Predictably, it was the cubs' presence and over-enthusiasm that would alert the impala and these hunts would fail.

It was also an excellent sign to see the young ones playing together frequently. On some occasions, I would see Furaha chasing in exaggerated bounds after a cub, tapping it left and right with her paws. Then she would playfully bite at its neck until the cub would turn on its back and raise its paws to defend itself vigorously. It was not uncommon on such occasions to see another cub rush in at speed and spring up on to Furaha's back, prompting her to leave the cub lying in front of her. Also on the few mercifully cooler mornings and evenings, when not accompanied by the cubs, the two mothers filled with bonhomie would play together like cubs themselves, ambushing and stalking each other. These were happy sights.

On my return, I went down to the Shashe and searched for signs of the missing cub, but found none. In the riverbed, though, I found tracks of where the lioness and the cubs had run and played exuberantly along the sand. It had been around full moon when this occurred and it must have been a magical and mesmerising sight — seven silver feline forms in silver light floating across the sands. As I thought of this, I thought too of the missing cub and my heart became heavy.

4

The Tale of Sticks

ONE late afternoon at the Tuli Safari Lodge, I saw the manageress approaching me and cupped in her hands was a tiny, wizened-faced baby monkey. After telling me that its mother was presumed dead and that the baby was found quite alone, she asked me whether Julie could care for him. I knew that Julie would love to do this and would try to ensure a future for the little chap. Additionally, caring for the baby would take Julie's mind off the troubled times. Julie, over the past two years, had already been foster mother to a porcupine called Nugu, a genet named Muna and many baby birds.

That night, travelling back with the baby in the open jeep, I muttered under my breath for the first of what were to be innumerable times in the future. I could not leave him on my lap as

I drove as he would probably have fallen off. I therefore put him under my T-shirt where I thought he could nestle. As I started the noisy engine, I felt the sharp pain of what seemed to be a hundred pinpricks on the centre of my chest. The little monkey was clinging with both hands and feet on to my chest hairs and he maintained this position for the entire drive.

The hour and a quarter journey through the bushlands at night (and through herd after herd of trumpeting elephants) was a torture. Additionally, whenever I slowed, I smelt a strong smell emanating from below me — but I tried not to think too much about its source. I was enormously pleased to eventually reach the camp's gate and when I got inside the camp, I extracted the monkey from my T-shirt and my chest hair. Unfortunately, that was not the only thing I extracted: smelly monkey excrement was spread liberally on me. I had not told Julie on the radio that I was bringing the baby, only telling her to expect a surprise. When I produced the tiny, mournful-eyed monkey who sucked at his fingers, she, in a maternal wave, whisked him from me and set about cleaning him. The word 'stinks' was used a lot by us that night, and somehow the word evolved to 'Sticks' which was what we christened him.

To be honest, I do not think Julie could have imagined how much attention and patience would be required to rear Sticks. Julie was not to get much sleep that night. Just prior to Sticks' arrival, after months of sleeping together in a small cramped tent, we had decided to spread out and sleep in separate places. We had cleaned out the small camp store room, moving equipment and boxes into two small dome tents. After much cleaning and sweeping, Julie was pleased with her (and what was to become Sticks') new abode — the first solid structure Julie had lived in for two and a half years.

On the second night of having Sticks at camp, I went to the old store room to say goodnight to the two of them. I saw a peaceful sight — Julie was snuggled on her stretcher and Sticks lay across her, fast asleep, sucking his fingers. The prognosis looked favourable for the two of them to have a good night's sleep. Unfortunately, this was not to be the case. Sticks at some point ended up on the floor whereupon he erupted into a most annoyed baby and his screams quickly woke Julie. After rescuing and reassuring him, Sticks then had a bowel movement — and quickly another major tantrum as Julie attempted to clean him and herself.

I was unaware of all this and the following day, I met a bleary-eyed Julie in the kitchen. She recounted to me the events of the night before. Looking around me, I asked her where Sticks was. She pointed to the store room. I went to it and looked in. There was Sticks peacefully asleep on Julie's pillow. I tiptoed away. Only minutes later, however, just as we had poured our tea, we heard his plaintive cries and rushed to the store room to collect and pacify him.

A few weeks later (during which time Sticks had well and truly 'adopted' Julie) and while I was away, Julie's mother visited her. One afternoon, as they were driving through the bushlands with Sticks asleep in Julie's mother's hands, they came across a huge elephant bull. It was calmly feeding and Julie slowed, then stopped to watch it. After a few minutes, Julie's mother lifted her hands (and Sticks) to window level. At that same time, Sticks stirred and opened his eyes to look sleepily around him. On seeing the elephant, his eyes bulged and he let out a piercing scream which startled Julie and her mother. He then leapt down on to the seat. He had never seen anything so large in all his life!

As he grew older, he became less dependent upon us and would explore his surroundings whether he was in the camp, in the vehicle or at one of his favourite places — the Botswana borderpost at Pont Drift. At camp, he would climb the trees, follow Julie around, and would take delight in rushing after any passing francolins or guineafowl which would, with an indignant bustle of feathers, flee. Sticks seemed, however, to have an incredibly high pain threshold as we noticed how he would scamper around seemingly unconcerned by little blisters on his hands and fingers. On seeing this, Julie would cut baby monkey-size plasters and put them on the heat blisters.

On journeys to the borderpost, he would climb out of the car window, if we did not manage to grab him in time, and go on to the roof, then suddenly appear on the windscreen in front of us. He would then disappear and would next be seen peering in the back window. At other times, like a sleepy human being, he would snuggle up and doze — normally next to or on a large gorilla soft toy he was very fond of. When waking up, he would climb on to the dashboard and watch with keen interest any animals we passed.

At the borderpost, we would leave him with our immigration and customs friends and continue on to South Africa. Sticks was not allowed to come with us due to regulations but also, as it was joked about at the border, because 'he has no passport'. At the borderpost, while waiting for us, he would play with the officials' children and would surprise both arriving and departing tourists by running up to them and grimacing. He was the borderpost mascot and loved by all.

It was at this time that the heat was becoming increasingly unbearable. We hauled out a shallow children's paddling pool we had been given. With shade temperatures in the forties, we would fill the pool with water and Julie and I would somehow squeeze in, desperately seeking a respite from the heat and we would encourage Sticks to join us. Sticks would initially watch us from the side then, getting bolder, he would lean forward with one of his elbows going into the water, but he would keep his fingers in his mouth. After seeing him do this several times, we realised that he was sucking water through his fur on to his hand and into his mouth. From then onwards, we had to try and deter him from this as his tummy would become bloated with water.

The day came when he voluntarily entered the water and sat with us — the heat becoming too much even for him. On one occasion, Julie and I were surprised to see him getting into the pool when we were not in it. We got a bigger surprise when, after sitting there for a while, he ducked himself completely under water and in an indescribable fashion swam the entire length along the bottom of the pool before surfacing, then hopping out, completely drenched. He performed this most un-monkey-like feat with great panache and dignity.

Sticks was very possessive of any items he came across and picked up and this created certain problems. For example, whenever I was attempting to repair one of our countless punctures, Sticks would initially sneak up behind me, then dash away with the tube of solution, or patches, or most irritating of all, the little tube valves. I might see him do this out of the corner of my eye and he would dash up a tree, perch there looking pleased with himself as I first cajoled, then raged below. I mentioned that most irritating of all was when he took the tube valves as these he would inevitably pop into his mouth. When I eventually got hold of him, it was tremendously difficult to extract them.

This possessiveness understandably

applied to any food Sticks had in his possession. He would eat what we did, but his overall diet was more varied than ours, supplemented by the insects, larvae and other foods he would search for around camp. Any attempts to go near him when he was eating would result in his dashing away clutching the food under his arm. Sometimes for Sticks, the best form of defence was attack on such occasions. This was demonstrated when Sticks and I had collected a visiting friend of mine from the border. My friend handed Sticks a long piece of dried boerewors (dried sausage), a food item he enjoyed immensely. As I drove, he perched himself on the dashboard, with his back to the windscreen and began to eat what was, in relation to his size, a substantial piece of boerewors. My friend was in high spirits about being in the bush and unfortunately as she chatted, she leant forward in play to tickle Sticks. He instantly saw red, fearing for his boerewors, and leapt directly off the dashboard, with the boerewors, on to her face. He gave her a good dig with his fingernails before leaping back to the dashboard with the boerewors still held protectively under his arm. He then turned his back to us and would turn his head to stare malevolently at my now low-spirited, somewhat shocked and slightly bloodied friend. Grimacing sheepishly, I told her it was too late to warn her that Sticks must not be interfered with when eating.

When Sticks got older, he unfortunately acquired a taste for white wine or, for that matter, any other alcoholic drink. I discovered him one day beside my sundowner drink, repeatedly dipping his fingers into the glass, then sucking at them. I yelled at him and he skipped away — but I think it was some time before this occasion that he had first sampled wine. From then onwards, we had to watch him carefully. On two occasions, he unfortunately drank considerable amounts without our knowledge. The first time, on seeing him under the influence, we were alarmed by his unco-ordinated movements. We then realised he was tipsy. On both occasions, he slept long and well, but upon waking, was seriously in pain from the alcohol's aftereffects — that is, he had a hangover. We felt so sorry for him as he held his head and attempted to roll over on to it to relieve the pain.

Each morning he would eat his portion of whatever breakfast we had, normally eating on top of the vehicle, staring philosophically at the rising sun — he was a slow starter in the mornings. In the evening, he would expectantly watch for the lions. He would inevitably spot them long before we did and would become excited. On their appearance, he would climb high on the camp fence and watch in horrified fascination as I moved amongst them as greeting ceremonies took place outside camp. Furaha and Rafiki were, I knew, very aware of his presence, but would pretend to ignore him. On bolder or rather less wise occasions, he would tease them by beginning to climb down the fence. He would dash back on top in a flourish whenever the lions could no longer ignore him and turned their heads to eye him.

Sticks simply disappeared one day when Julie was away. I was going about my work and at some point noticed he was missing. I called and called his name, then went out into the bush around the camp looking for him. After about two hours of searching, I felt a heaviness in my heart. I went back to camp to check there, then searched again. When I returned to camp the second time and he was not there, I began to search for his tracks which might give an indication as to where he had left the camp, but his tracks were everywhere and this was largely unsuccessful. I thought perhaps a snake had taken him or a bird of prey and looked for signs of this, but fortunately found none. I hoped, considering the situation, that perhaps he had been picked up by a passing family of monkeys. This was very possible as other monkeys always took great interest in him and in fact, on two occasions, we had tried to introduce him into two separate troops. On both occasions, the families, I felt, would have accepted him, but he would show no interest in joining them. I prayed that a female had snatched him away and that he would adapt to being in the wilds amongst his own kind. His disappearance left a gap in our lives, but we tried to be positive, hoping he was with a monkey family.

A few weeks later, an incident occurred that made us believe that this was the case. I was driving with a friend near camp when suddenly I saw a troop of monkeys near the road to camp. My friend, who was unaware of the situation, must have thought I had gone completely bush mad when I braked suddenly and jumped out of the vehicle calling, 'Sticks, Sticks'. The monkeys fled and I surmised that he was not with them. I then turned to my friend and began to tell him the tale of Sticks. Suddenly, as I was about to close the car door, I saw a young monkey of Sticks's size coming towards me at speed. Then, in a flash, it was grabbed by an adult female who suddenly materialised. The youngster instinctively held her as she turned and dashed away. Over the months ahead, further incidents indicated that he was indeed back with those of his own kind.

5

Praying for Rain

THE Tuli Lion Trust's anti-poaching team, which had done so much good work, had only been up and running for nine months when it was, in effect, taken over by the Charter Reserve Management. I was told by one of the landowners that it did not reflect well upon them in the eyes of the government that such conservation work (which they should have been implementing) was being undertaken by us, independents, and not landowners. I did not have much choice in the matter when I handed over the responsibility of our anti-poaching team to the Charter Reserve. I did this with reservations as I feared for the future effectiveness of the team. I attempted to make it a proviso that our men's work be maintained on a full-time basis, that they would patrol daily and that they would never be taken off patrolling to do other work. Anti-poaching is only effective if it is undertaken constantly and consistently.

Initially, their effectiveness in the bush remained unchanged, but then standards began to slip when gradually they were pulled off their anti-poaching work to do other jobs. In time, they were also taken off anti-poaching to do building jobs at the warden's base. I felt this was grossly unfair. Poaching was now allowed to go unchecked as my staff even had to build their own accommodation at their new base. More and more, they were doing other work because of the warden's staff shortage — or rather, due to the lack of money made available to the warden to undertake work such as improvements to the landowners' camps. The warden said that unfortunately, if special attention was not given to the landowners' camps, there would probably not be a wardenship at all. Outside the Charter portion of the area, the situation was even worse with virtually no anti-poaching schemes taking place in the rest of the bushlands.

Because of this grave situation, I

began to put much of my work aside to concentrate on spending long hours patrolling on foot for poachers and their snares. I was patrolling an area of some 100 square kilometres on my own. It was exhausting work, particularly as now Christmas drew close, our mid-summer, and shade temperatures were soaring into the thirties by mid-morning, and into the upper forties from midday onwards. I had no permission from the landowners to be on much of the land I patrolled — but as no one else patrolled there, ironically my presence went completely undetected — just as a poacher's presence would have gone unnoticed if I had not been patrolling and checking.

Each morning in what turned out to be week after week, I would either drive out to an area and then set out on foot, or alternatively start from camp, depending on which part of the bushlands I needed to check. For a year, I had no rifle available to me (the cost of buying a firearm was prohibitive) and I patrolled armed with only a spear, which one day I had found in the bush, left years ago, I suspect, by a poacher. In my other hand, I carried a *panga* (machete). Fortunately, due to our poacher-deterrent presence over the previous two years in the Pitsani and Tawana valleys, the lions' core area, I would find very few signs of new poaching activity and occasionally would find old snares. But this situation would only be maintained as long as I patrolled the area frequently.

Along the Shashe river, however, there was cause for concern as I would come across new snares. The physical exertion and worry took its toll on me at this time, and writing this reminds me of a time of equally hot days and hot nights, and long patrolling when my resistance was undoubtedly low. I developed a nasty abcess near my lower intestine; it was literally a pain in the butt which I can joke about today, but which nevertheless was a cause for concern at the time.

Against Julie's wishes and warnings, I stubbornly and very foolishly refused to leave the area, the lions and the need for anti-poaching patrols, to seek medical attention. I had experienced something similar in the past. At that time prescribed antibiotics had not worked, and the abcess grew until one night it finally burst after which in time it healed. As the abcess grew this time, so did the pain. The night it erupted was one of the most painful I have ever experienced. The abcess at that point felt the size of a small orange and pain killers did little to alleviate what I was feeling. Julie stayed beside me in the tent that night and I took deep swallows from a bottle of whisky and gritted my teeth.

At about 1.00 a.m., Julie heard me suddenly moan, saw me writhe in pain and then I screamed as the wretched thing finally burst. She later told me that the appalling smell of the fluid was indescribable. The pus drained from me. It was a grotesque experience for both of us. Later, after swabbing away the fluid and as the whisky finally took hold, I slept. Over the following days, the abcess drained completely and I quickly got back to patrolling — much to Julie's criticism and annoyance. My obsession with keeping the lions' range free of snares might seem excessive — but I was so worried that if I did not maintain a vigilant presence, a tragedy would occur. What would a parent not do to prevent the possible death of its child? My situation with the lions was exactly the same — one of a parent with all the fears that go with parenthood.

★ ★ ★

On occasions on these foot patrols, I would find spoor of my lions which I would sometimes follow, then after meeting up with them, I would sit a while amongst them before continuing. The pride was now spending more time in their old core area. This was due in part to Zimmale having moved south and was associating with the remnants of the Lower Majale pride, but also because two lionesses with six cubs, of almost identical age to those of Furaha and Rafiki, had moved south from the Tuli Safari Area and were occupying the top Shashe region. The presence of this group denied my pride access to the perennial water and abundant prey of the Shashe, because they wanted to avoid the other lion group.

A major problem for my pride now

was that within the Tawana and Pitsani Valleys, natural water levels were at a record low. Rain had still not fallen and for the first time, I witnessed the Pitsani waterpoint totally drying up on the surface. Where in past years, whatever the climatical conditions, water could always been found, now all that could be seen was a baked depression. In desperation, at this once perennial water point and at the barely surviving ones further down the river, I would dig with a pick and shovel down to the water level, and thus allow the water to seep upwards. But as the days passed, the level got lower until at the top waterpoint, I could not, because of bedrock, reach down far enough to create a viable seep for the animals.

At the lower water point, I would almost daily come across a depressing sight. A baboon troop would be present, drinking in turn in social hierarchy at the seeps. Because replenishment was so slow, they would have to spend most of the day there and foraged for only a fraction of what they normally would. They were becoming incredibly thin and my heart went out to them.

Every other day, I would go down to the seeps and dig deeper and wider for them, and the other animals. The elephants which would have normally undertaken this role in normal years (thus assisting other species) were congregated where their great thirst could be more easily slaked — along the Shashe and Limpopo where pools still existed — and so the Pitsani seeps shrank. Initially, upon my arrival, the baboons would shriek and flee away. But as the days passed, they became incredibly used to my presence and I felt they knew what I was doing. Upon my appearance, the troop members would move to sit quietly to one side, but after I had opened one seep and moved to another, there would be a mad rush past me to the water. These baboons, which ran scared and panicked just days before, would sit only metres away while I dug and scooped. I grew very fond of them. I would sit afterwards watching them and inevitably, turn my head skywards and think of rain.

Returning to the lionesses, the combination of decreased prey in this core area due to the lack of luring waters, the extreme heat, plus the responsibility of fending for the five cubs, took a toll upon them. The cubs always looked full and healthy. The lionesses, I saw, contrary to other people's observations on lionesses and their cubs, put their little ones first when food was available and of this I will write further. Furaha and Rafiki lost weight, but retained their fitness. Zimmale occasionally moved north and absconded with kills at this time which did not help matters. The conditions that summer were punishing to man and beast, and from the water in drums which we brought to camp for all our needs, a portion would always be used to keep the lions drinking drums full. At least, they always knew there would be water to drink near camp.

I felt their struggle deeply. They and we were sapped by the harsh conditions in the bush. Daily, we would watch as clouds and even thunderheads would build up in the south. The heat would radiate everywhere and all around — in the open beaks of hot birds, in the brittle scrape of a branch. There were cries for rain. Mopane flies, small black stingless bees, would crowd into eyes and nostrils and around the mouths of humans and the lions as they sought moisture. Julie and I, on particularly blasting hot days, would witness small birds crowding into shaded parts of the camp — even shade temperatures would be in the forties — the conditions making them fearless of us. In some other camps, some birds died of the heat and a snake allegedly died on contact when hitting the heat of the ground after being frightened from a low bush by a policeman friend of mine.

One particularly oppressive day on patrol remains strongly in my mind. I was plodding along on patrol north of camp. I would occasionally stop to look south, willing the thunderheaded clouds in our direction. Mopane bees repeatedly entered my eyes, swarming around my head, and many stuck to my hair beside my perspiring scalp. As I trudged out and up the Pitsani Valley, I suddenly saw in the distance five golden forms and to the right heard the alarm snorts of impala. It was the cubs and they had been seen.

Furaha and Rafiki were hidden, closing in on the herd, but the cubs in youthful and unstifled enthusiasm had advanced also. I then saw a lioness appear from the stream bed and heard her moan deeply. It was Rafiki. I recognised her even at this distance because whenever a kill attempt failed, she would moan to herself forlornly. I moved closer then and sat upon a rock. I called to her and she looked up and turned to come to me. In the heart and heat of the bushlands, we greeted, bonding in our fellowship, then she lay on the ground resting with me.

I then saw Furaha way in the distance. She turned in my direction and called once in greeting as she led the cubs away. I looked down at Rafiki. She was thin and bubbles of spittle lined the soft black edges of her mouth. 'Poor Fiks', I thought to myself. The mopane flies plagued her eyes and mine. She then rose and together we walked back in the direction from which she had come. Upon reaching the stream bed, I saw the tracks of Furaha and the cubs. They were somewhere ahead. Rafiki and I headed on. I looked to the south again and the clouds had definitely advanced in our direction. I prayed silently that tonight the rain would come and a reprieve for the bushlands would occur.

We walked on for a while before I saw Rafiki move to the right, then peer into a shepherd's tree. I gripped my spear, fearing that amongst the canopy was a leopard with its prey hidden aloft in the branches. I looked closely, but saw no leopard, only its long-deserted prey — the dried remains of an impala. Rafiki leapt into the tree and began pulling at the carcass. She was very hungry. Finally she hooked it loose and I saw it fall like a bundle of dry sticks to the ground. As it struck the ground, I heard in the distance the sound of hundreds of hooves thundering across the higher ground to the west. 'Furaha hunting', I thought and upon seeing the dried maggot-cleaned carcass in front of me, I said quietly, 'Kill, Furaha. Kill one so that you and Rafiki can eat.' Rafiki dropped to the ground and began gnawing at the pathetic remains of the impala.

I left Rafiki and did not seek Furaha. I hoped she had killed and did not wish to disturb her. Feast, famine, eland, wizened remains of another predator's feast. Such was the pendulum swing in the drought that sucked the land dry, sucking too the energy of those that lived in this harsh land. I headed away south, my mind hazy from the heat and glare. The mopane flies sucked at my eyes and the dead ones left a sour smell in my hair — but I noticed that the clouds in the south were moving towards me.

As the sun began to set, sweat still poured off me and the ground still radiated heat. Above me, the sky was completely clear, all the flirting clouds of promise had now departed. It was to be yet another warm night and the next day, the heat would build up once again. It was a time that made you feel as though half of yourself was dead and the other half did not care.

Summer nights are times of snakes and scorpions and at our camp, the deadliest of each slid and scurried — puff adders and cobras, and of the scorpion specie, the thick-tailed neuro-toxic parabuthis. One hot night, I awoke to piercing screams. I froze, attempting to locate the sounds and to identify their source.

The direction of the sounds I realised as my sleep-buffered mind cleared, was directly beneath my head — eighteen inches or so below my stretcher on the ground. I turned on my torch and shone it cautiously. There I saw a puff adder, marked typically with black half moons upon its wide back. Grasped in its mouth was a twitching mouse. I knew that mouse. It had lived in my tent and for months would scurry at night, busy with its nocturnal foraging, and by day, it would sleep amongst my clothes in the old wardrobe. We hated to kill anything, but for our own safety had to draw the line at venomous snakes and scorpions in the camp. I seized a rock that I kept in my tent. I called it 'Batian's stone', a rock he would often rest against in earlier times. At my movement, the puff adder dropped its prey and slid heavily across the tent floor. I threw 'Batian's stone' at it. It died and I felt remorse . . .

Just after this incident, Julie woke early one morning after a frightening dream about a snake. While I slept on, she made tea and then headed in the pre-dawn light to bring me a cup. She heard a sound in the grass near where I had dragged my stretcher the previous evening to seek cooler air. Hearing the sound, she was reminded of her dream and stopped before cautiously making a wide detour towards me. As she reached my sleeping form, she felt something wet on her bare thighs and saw minute droplets of liquid. She woke me, telling hurriedly of her dream, the sound in the grass and of the droplets. 'Cobra,' I said groggily, 'Spitting cobra.' We wiped the venom away and waited for the sun to appear over the horizon. Then together, armed with sticks, we inspected the place where she had stopped on hearing the rustles. I then saw the passing of a large snake, the smooth curves of its passage upon the grey soft powdery dust. It had spat at Julie before moving away. Luckily, the venom had hit her legs. Normally, the black-necked spitting cobra aims at the reflection in one's eyes. Upon hitting its target, the venom causes excruciating pain and without prompt treatment results in eye damage and degrees of blindness.

It was just after Julie's cobra incident

that I was given the use of a fine rifle by a friend, Inspector Nxane of the Botswana Police Force. He said to me one day while visiting Tawana, 'It's enough now. You cannot continue to do what you do without the protection of a rifle. I want you to use mine.' Very gratefully, I accepted his offer and carried his rifle on my anti-poaching patrols for the following six months until his retirement from the Force, after which he returned to his home in northern Botswana.

Prior to Inspector Nxane coming to the rescue with the loan of his rifle, we had had no firearm protection in the bushlands for an entire year. I had been unbelievably fortunate in that a fatal incident had not occurred. Bearing this in mind, it was strange that just a week after receiving the rifle, an incident did take place that I feel could have resulted in my death if I had been armed only with my old spear and *panga*.

Early one morning, Julie and I were driving on the plateau country above Poachers' Valley searching for the pride which we had not seen for some days. I found spoor of two lionesses and a mess of cub spoor. All the signs indicated that they were those of my pride and I proceeded to track on foot while Julie drove a little distance behind me. We did this for a quarter of an hour until the country became impassable for the vehicle. The decline ahead was steep and blocked by thickets of mopane scrub which led to the valley leading towards the Shashe. I discussed with Julie how I would continue tracking ahead on foot and we agreed that I would meet her back at the vehicle after a while.

I had an uneasy feeling, but could not pinpoint why. The spoor I was following indicated, both in number and in sizes, that it was that of my pride. I shrugged the disquiet away and continued onwards. I followed the tracks down the valley, losing it several times on the stony slopes. It led me into the centre of the valley, the stream bed, and I walked on, following for about a kilometre until suddenly the tracks led off up on to the stream bank.

I inspected the spoor and then heard a movement ahead of me. I saw cubs thirty metres away, scuttling off just as Furaha and Rafiki's cubs would do whenever I appeared unexpectedly in the bush. In a split second, I heard the loud enraged bellow of adult lions and saw two lionesses fifteen metres apart launch themselves forward and rush headlong down the bank towards me. I shouted at them as I quickly loaded the rifle, then fired a shot into the ground at a point ahead of the lionesses as they bounded side by side towards me. Stones scattered as the bullet hit the ground and both lionesses came to a standstill. I stepped back, reloading, and amidst outraged growls, I moved out of their sight, backing further and further away into the mopane scrub.

Safely distanced from the lionesses, I cursed myself for walking into and upsetting what was clearly not my pride but that of the newly established Shashe lionesses — this being the first time that I had actually seen them. I made a wide half-circle detour back towards the vehicle, ensuring that I remained out of their sight.

Meanwhile, at the vehicle, Julie was tense. She had seen me disappear, then many minutes later, she had heard the lions' bellows, my shouts, then the single shot. Then all was quiet except for ominous growls. She made a decision and got out of the vehicle, calling my name repeatedly. Sound sometimes carries strangely in the bush. Julie had obviously heard the commotion, yet I did not hear her calls. Julie has a brave heart and, convinced that an attack had occurred, she seized my large hunting knife in one hand, the *panga* in the other, and began cautiously venturing down the valley in search of me. Fortunately she had not gone far when I spotted her and called her name. Relief poured from her as she turned and saw me. Her hands wielding the knife and the *panga* fell to her sides. I went to her and put my arm around her shoulder and together we headed back to the vehicle.

★ ★ ★

The torturous season of drought continued and these words from Julie's diary sum up the situation well: 'No rain for almost two months and the temperatures are between 45° – 50° every day. Nobody could live with this permanently. The Pitsani waterpoints are just mud; the animals barely move from their shady spots when we drive past in the heat of the day.'

6

To a New Tawana

THE reduction in anti-poaching patrolling meant that I had to continue patrolling — the sole anti-poaching presence in some 100 square kilometres of the Tuli bushlands — over the hot Christmas and New Year period. Those long foot patrols, however tiring, were generally (and fortunately) quiet times. On occasions, though, dangerous situations arose — and then there were times when I witnessed the extraordinary.

On one particularly danger-filled patrol, I had two separate encounters with leopards, a pride of lions, a herd of elephant and, lastly, a black mamba — which in anyone's book must be considered excessive!

I had set out early to the high ground to the west and continued down into Poachers' Valley heading towards the great sand river of the Shashe. When I was some four kilometres from the Shashe camp, I suddenly saw in a huge leadwood tree a feline shape silhouetted against the bright morning light. It was a large male leopard. I stopped and saw it leap quickly down to the ground. I shouted and raised my rifle in readiness to let off a warning shot as it seemed to turn and head towards me. The blinding light obscured my vision, but after many seconds of tension, I lowered my rifle, thinking I had been mistaken and I continued on, detouring around where I had last seen the leopard. Upon reaching the Shashe camp, I spoke to Jippy, a mild-mannered Tswana friend of mine, who was an excellent tracker. He worked at this camp and I asked him whether he had seen any sign of lions. He replied that that morning, just before sunrise, a pride of two lionesses and cubs had passed through the vicinity of the camp and had headed towards Poachers' Valley. Jippy was surprised that I had not seen the pride's spoor earlier in the valley and suggested that we track them. The spoor initially, as we followed it, indicated to us that it was my pride — but I became worried. The charge by the Shashe lionesses had occurred only weeks before and this had taught me to no longer assume that spoor of lionesses and cubs in the Shashe was necessarily that of my pride.

The lion spoor led us close to where I had encountered the leopard and Jippy and I left the spoor to determine whether indeed the leopard had rushed at me just an hour or so previously. Below the grey-boughed benign old leadwood, we saw in the dust where the leopard had hit the ground and to where it had indeed bounded in long earth-biting bounds towards me. We followed and saw where it had slammed to a standstill (presumably because of my shout) and to the right where it had dashed away towards the stream bed. Jippy eyed me shyly and said quietly, 'You were very lucky, Gareth.' I nodded. I had not clearly seen the silent rush of the leopard and had not known because of the obscuring blinding sun how close a call the encounter had in fact been.

We continued along the pride's spoor

with Jippy leading. Fifteen minutes later, he stopped and whistled, nodding his head in surprise as he pointed at the ground. There in front of us were my own tracks and across and on top of them were the spoor of lions! They had obviously been very close as I came along the valley and, after I passed, had crossed where I had walked. We had just missed encountering each other.

Jippy and I then climbed on to a hillside and I felt the lions were close. I cautioned Jippy to stay some distance behind as I searched ahead to where I could scan down the hillside for the pride. As I reached the hill's edge, I heard a movement below, followed by the high piercing growl of a lioness down amongst the trees — I knew immediately these were not my lions and I stepped quietly backwards to where I had left Jippy. In a low voice, I told him it was not my pride but that of the Shashe and we crept away heading towards his camp.

Only a kilometre further along, we came across a large elephant herd moving in our direction. Due to a difficult shifting breeze, we had to carefully manoeuvre around the herd and at one point had to sprint quickly at an angle past them. A few of the herd caught our scent and raised their trunks. We managed to remain relatively undetected though and briskly made our way to the camp, hearing the occasional trumpeting of elephants behind us.

This indeed was an eventful patrol and the dangerous encounters did not end there. While we were smoking cigarettes at the camp, Jippy told me how during the night before, he thought he had heard lions making a kill in the dense riverine bush not far from his hut. Stubbing out our cigarettes, we decided to investigate and headed away. We soon came across the scant remains of five goats, unfortunate members of a herd that had crossed the Shashe from the Zimbabwean livestock area.

After inspecting the remains and the Shashe pride's spoor, we patrolled along the river bank in search of poachers' snares. In a particularly thick area, in the space of two minutes or so, startling things happened. First, we both heard a rustle in a mashatu tree a few yards from us and, upon spinning around, we saw a small leopard fall heavily to the ground. It sped away, crashing through the undergrowth. Then, just a few steps later, with our hearts drumming, Jippy hissed a warning to me and I leapt high to one side as I saw a thick, long black mamba, Africa's most feared snake, slither past, its coffin-shaped head raised partially off the ground in alertness.

After this, our nerves felt severely overtaxed. We checked for snares, then I bade Jippy goodbye and, taking the most risk-free route upon hilltops, I struck out alone back to camp. There I told Julie of my encounter-filled patrol and I wondered how close my guardian spirit had been that morning. I think he must have been nearby as once again I was totally unharmed and in one piece.

One of the most extraordinary sights I have ever encountered on patrol occurred just a few weeks later. One mid-morning, I came across, deep within their territory, the spoor of my lions and followed it to the place where I saw they had dug open much of a warthog burrow. On closer inspection, I discovered a macabre sight. I saw the head of a dead female warthog protruding from the hard ground. Her body from the neck downwards was jammed tight underground in the burrow. I pulled at her head, but could not dislodge her. I then walked to a camp where I had left my jeep and returned to the burrow with another tracker friend of mine whose name is Bingo.

On approaching the burrow, Bingo's lynx-sharp eyes spotted more lion spoor and he pointed out where these tracks led towards a separate burrow system some 100 metres away from that of the warthog. We left the jeep and walked up to the burrow. Inside it, we saw a thick, almost hairless tail, like that of a gigantic rat — a tail we both recognised to be that of an aardvark.

Bingo's hunting instincts, which at times I noticed were as sharp as those of a lion, took over when he saw the tail. He quickly bent down and seized the tail. The aardvark's reaction was dramatic with Bingo very nearly being pulled into the burrow. Aardvarks are immensely powerful diggers, possessing long, thick dirt-ploughing claws. It is with these claws that they break open termite mounds in search of these tiny beings that constitute a large percentage of their diet.

Bingo let go of the aardvark and together, we listened to the grinding noise as the aardvark continued burrowing beneath us. The ground, I must add, was almost rock hard, baked by the long days of hot sun and no rain. The sounds became fainter, then we heard another sound some four yards ahead of us. As we looked up, we saw an extraordinary sight. The baked ground erupted like a small volcano, the aardvark materialised from the ground and dashed away. This was again too much for Bingo's honed hunting instincts and I chuckled as I saw him charge past me after the aardvark, but it outran him and disappeared down another burrow.

On Bingo's return, we walked over to the warthog burrow. Together, we pulled at the female's head, but despite our straining and collective tugging, we could not dislodge her. I then resorted to bringing the jeep in and, after tying

116

an old snare around the warthog's head with the other end tied to the vehicle, with much wheel slipping and high revs, I managed to tow the warthog's body from the hole.

As I switched off the jeep's motor, I heard Bingo muttering as he peered into the hole. Then I saw the reason for his astonishment. Packed into the cavity were a set of dead piglets, behind which was their dead father. It was an appalling sight and the horror of what had transpired occurred to Bingo and I as we hauled the bodies out.

The night before, the lions, led by scent, had discovered the warthog family asleep deep within the burrow. Then they had spent a lot of time attempting to dig the warthogs out. They had excavated much of the burrow's underground system and by retreating, the warthogs had become packed into the remaining space with the female facing outwards to the pride. There she had been killed by the grip of one of the lions to her muzzle but the lions, as had happened to me, had been quite unable to dislodge her. No doubt, with reluctance and frustration and having then become tired, they had moved away. Inside the burrow, oxygen was running out in the airtight cavity and, in time and most horribly, the piglets and their father had suffocated and died. This was a most bizarre and cruel encounter between predator and prey — one that had left the lions, after expending much energy, without food and one that resulted in the deaths of the entire warthog family.

Ever opportunistic when meat was available, Bingo set about cutting some portions off the adult warthog, loading them next to the piglets which I had collected to give to Rafiki and Furaha should they by chance visit the camp that evening. By coincidence, that late afternoon, the pride did indeed come to the camp. After our greetings, I began handing them the piglets, and I wondered to myself whether they would recognise where they came from. I then witnessed another unusual sight. After taking a piglet each, both lionesses walked to the cubs and gave them the food selflessly instead of fuelling their own bodies. This they repeated until I had handed them the final piglets. The cubs fed noisily, swatting and growling at each other as I sat with their mothers, watching them in the twilight.

* * *

The drought continued, a dreadful season of torturing dryness, a season in which less than 100 mm of rain would fall, a third of the annual meagre rainfall. Increasingly, I was receiving reports of lions being drawn towards tourist camps, attracted by the herds of prey heading to drink at the artificial waterholes at the camps. Antelope from miles around trod the game trails that, like the spokes of a wheel's hub, led to where water was being pumped. The thousands of hooves etched the red-earthed trails until they became like narrow furrows. It was reported that my pride were also seen at night at these unfenced camps and I feared for them. I knew that under normal circumstances, they would not pose a danger to people, but I feared that people, acting irrationally or without an understanding of lion behaviour, could pose a threat to them.

The camps were unfenced, which meant a tourist could walk out of a tent at night (despite being warned not to) and stumble into my lions or any other predator. Old Darky, months before, had killed a kudu antelope right up against one of the tourist tents. When the camp was first established, a tragedy almost occurred. A ranger colleague of mine was asleep in his tent with his fiancée when suddenly he awoke to her screams. His fiancée had been seized by a hyaena which had quite simply walked into their tent. The ranger kicked and shouted at the hyaena and successfully forced it to let go of her. It had been pulling her out of the tent into the night. Fortunately, she did not sustain serious injury, but her shock was tremendous, surviving an attack that would have otherwise resulted in a most terrifying death.

Another of my colleagues, a bird expert, sustained an attack, again by a hyaena, in an unfenced camp. This time, it was not in the bushlands, but in an army camp in the Kruger National Park. Roger, who is a well-built, amiable fellow was asleep in a tent when a hyaena attacked. Roger's bush instincts, I feel, saved his life as he awoke just as the most powerful jaws in Africa were lunging forward. He swung his head to one side and the hyaena glanced his skull and bit off his left ear. Roger hit out and his shouts brought help — and the hyaena loped away. It was never seen again, and probably is still out there somewhere in the bush. Roger suffered days and weeks of awful infection from his neck upwards, but fortunately recovered and bravely returned to the bush where he worked with me in the Tuli.

On hearing the reports of the lions in the vicinity of camps, I wrote to the Landowners' Association with suggestions as to how potential conflict between animals and man could be reduced. I advised them to put up fences around the camps, fences that do not have to be noticeable to tourists or aesthetically unpleasing, but which would ensure protection of people, and the animals. I also suggested that vegetable gardens at camps should not be established as these inevitably attract baboons and vervet monkeys, who then get shot for raiding. In one camp in the bushlands, spring hares, those delightful rodents that hop by night like miniature kangaroos, were being shot for feeding upon garden lawns. It seems that whenever a camp is established in the bush, a lawn follows — lawns like those in towns. It was wrong that the spring hares, in the midst of the debilitating drought, were shot dead for feeding upon the planted and much watered grass. In other camps, I have known staff to be ordered to kill squirrels which make nests in thatch roofs. Such occurrences angered me and illustrated the lack of respect for the real residents of the bushlands — the animals.

In a verbal reply to my suggestions on reducing animal/human conflict, I was told shortly, with particular reference to fencing, 'Of course we have no authority to tell our members [members of the Landowners' Association] how to spend their money.' I felt lives were worth more than rich men's money and in the weeks ahead, I provided fencing for friends of mine, staff members of three different camps, who had previously had to live in unfenced, unprotected 'compounds'.

★ ★ ★

At this time, I had the arduous task of breaking down Tawana, our home. The end of the lease period was looming and the lease was not going to be renewed. I was relieved that Julie was away much of this time as the process of knocking down one's home is heartbreaking. We had been invited to establish a new base in the extreme north west by a syndicate of landowners, and although we were most grateful for their offer, ideally we did not want to live outside the lions' range. To protect them (apart from my patrolling, when only erratic anti-poaching work was taking place), I needed to remain within their 200 square kilometre range — an area in human terms which encompassed portions of land owned by seven different landowners.

With Julie away, wall by wall, pole by pole, I brought the camp down — moving much of the rubble upstream of the Tawana. Some day, someone would find it there. One morning, while working, I heard the sound of angry snarling coming from the direction to which I was taking the rubble. I feared that a predator had been caught in a snare. Three days earlier I had seen human footprints in that area and fearing it was poachers, I had searched for snares, but found none. I instantly thought of the footprints and headed out with Inspector Nane's rifle to investigate. As I passed the pile of rubble, I heard the snarling again and it came from a circle of tall trees upon the stream bank. I entered cautiously fearing an animal was distressed, but the only thing in trouble was me. Unbelievably, before my eyes, I saw two mating leopards! The male saw me and leapt off the female, rushing towards me before tearing away. The female quickly followed. With my heart drumming I stood there watching where they had gone. Then I stepped backward out into the more open bush. My good intentions had very nearly ended up with myself being in trouble. The male leopard could have so easily followed through with his charge instead of breaking off to flee.

I had once again been very fortunate indeed.

Back at the camp, I continued with the depressing work. With a sledgehammer, I would slam against the concrete walls — first the mess hut came down, then the kitchen and finally Julie's bedroom, the old store room. For hours, I sweated as my muscles strained. I was determined that if we had to leave no one else would live here again. It had been a special home for Julie and me, one where there had been laughter and tears, a place where nearby we had buried Batian. But as I worked, the familiar became mere memories. When, in the days ahead, I left Tawana to set up the new camp, I blocked the road with branches and logs to deter the curious from driving in to see what remained of our home.

Fortunately, a sympathetic landowner to the east of the Tawana Valley had granted me permission to site a new camp on his neighbouring land, for which I was relieved and grateful. I knew the area well as it was deep within the lions' central territory and one afternoon, I set out to look for a new site where I would erect a new base camp. I was drawn to a high plateau area, probably the highest point in all the bushlands, which had sweeping views down the ancient Limpopo valley where the dense green riverine trees bordered the sand river. To the west was a plain, and beyond it were the Tawana and Pitsani valleys. I could see the north-western lands and, on the horizon, tiny dots which were in fact gigantic baobab trees, dwarfed by the immensity of the landscape. I was drawn to this beautiful spot in part because it was here where Rafiki had led Batian and me many months before. She had led us to a secret place where she had given birth to a single cub, who sadly had been stillborn.

As I walked around the new site, picturing and planning how the camp would look, I was surprised to discover right there the spoor of my pride — and I wondered whether this was coincidence.

During the days that followed, I loaded our belongings on to the pick-up truck and took them to the new site. Exhausted in the evenings, I would sit next to the ruin of Julie's room and there amongst the ghosts of the camp, I would cook supper on my old paraffin stove.

The lions visited me at this time only very occasionally, and I was glad of that. I did not wish them to sense, as they would, what I felt. But early one evening, Rafiki appeared alone at the camp and, for the first time, I saw a lion expressing emotional pain. She felt my hurt, I believe, and as she stared in at the ruins she called in a strange mournful way. I went to her and a rumble of pain reverberated from deep within her. I feel she was reacting in part to my own emotions — but perhaps to more. She was clearly distressed, perhaps feeling that I was going to depart for ever.

Just prior to the final move, the entire pride paid one of their now rare visits. It was to be the last time that I would see all five cubs and the two lionesses together. It was evening, as I sat in the darkness, I heard the gate rattle loudly. When I went to investigate, I saw the lions there. I felt that Zimmale might be near, perhaps further down the valley as whenever he was in the area, my pride would never announce their presence with their usual calls. They would as they did that night push against the gate or the fence. I stepped out of the gate and became as one amongst them.

After that evening, I only saw Rafiki and Furaha with two cubs. I named them Sala and Tana. Both cubs' names are synonymous with George Adamson and his beloved Kora Reserve. 'Tana' is the name of the large river which forms the reserve's northern boundary. 'Sala' is the name of a dry 'sand' river which leads and joins the Tana. Slightly larger, Sala was Rafiki's while Tana, a particularly beautiful little female, was Furaha's daughter. I never discovered what had caused the disappearance of the other three cubs, but it seems all were lost at the same time and I feel it is possible that Zimmale committed infanticide. They were almost nine months' old when they died, up to their mothers' chins in height and they would have weighed approximately 30 kgs at that age.

I pondered on the cubs' disappearance and wondered if they would still be alive and with the pride if Batian had not been killed. Batian, as pride male, would have given his sisters' pride the security which is so essential to lion society. Were the cubs' deaths therefore not an extension of Batian's? I felt they were and this angered me further. This unbalanced situation was occurring throughout the Tuli. With the remaining prides and without the security of the pride males, cub mortality would inevitably rise and conflict with hyaena clans would intensify. This downward spiral for lion society is inflicted by man and will continue until man rises to the moral responsibility of promoting stability by affording protection for lions in the bushlands.

★ ★ ★

As I was alone without any staff, the process of establishing a fenced-off new camp area, complete with long drop toilet (a deep dark hole in the ground with planks laid across the top, and adorned with the upside-down elephant jawbone we used as a toilet seat), would have been a long one if it had not been for the generous help of my Tswana friends. At the Hatari camp, owned by the sympathetic landowner and his partners, lived four of my friends — Bingo, of whom I have already written, tall and rangy Petrus, the camp caretaker, my old friend Philemon, a roof thatcher by trade, and his assistant, Suna, one of my former anti-poaching guards. They gave up their weekend to pull down the 12-foot fence and poles surrounding the one-acre old campsite, and put up the fencing and poles in a similarly sized area at the new site. The men worked like Trojans. On the first day, we pulled down most of the fencing and necessary poles, transported them to the 'new' Tawana, dug the foundation holes and set the poles in concrete so that the fencing could be attached the following day.

That night, after my friends had returned to Hatari camp for the night, a strange occurrence took place. Just after sunset, I sat in the fenceless camp amongst the piles of roofing sheets and camp equipment. I worried that the lions might arrive at the old Tawana camp and I pondered on what their reaction would be if they arrived there to find the camp empty and ruined.

The sky darkened and I thought of them and of Julie, and of the unknown future based in this new place. I felt very alone. Then I heard a familiar low call nearby. At first, I did not believe that I had heard the call. Then the call again floated towards me and I stood up. In the twilight, I saw my pride, with Rafiki leading, heading slowly towards me. My heart surged. Somehow they had sensed where I was and had come to me. I greeted them almost in tears. I may have been forced to leave our original home and had moved away, but the lions had sensed this and had found me. It was extraordinary.

Later that night, the pride moved with me to my old tent. I sat there on a seat and both lionesses lay contentedly at my feet as the cubs, Sala and Tana, peered shyly behind them on the hill's edge. Incredible calmness and a sense of peace prevailed. A storm began to build up in the distant north and as it rumbled, the lions rose and filed away into the night streaked by lightning. I no longer felt alone.

Early the following day, my friends

arrived to help me put up the camp fencing. Their faces showed complete astonishment as I told them the lions had found me. They saw this for themselves when they looked down at the lion spoor where they now stood. As I did, they too thought it was a wondrous thing.

By five o'clock that afternoon, the fencing was complete. It was only six feet high, half the size of that at the old camp, and due to the haste with which we had erected it, it was not as secure. But with the kind help of my friends I had a new Tawana. It was without a single solid building and was many times more rugged than the original camp, but it was a home and somewhere for Julie and me to continue with our work.

On Julie's return from South Africa, we began to build a makeshift mess area beside a shepherd's tree which, during the afternoons in the weeks ahead, would cast mercifully dense shade over where we worked at the long table. Additionally, we erected the scaffolding, the lookout post, and from the top of it, we had an unparalleled view of the bushlands. We would sit up there in the late afternoons viewing the landscape and the animals below.

Coming back to the old camp gone and the new one set up was difficult for Julie. The situation she was familiar with had changed. She felt it was not really her home, but more my camp. She had been away for several long periods and on her return now felt somewhat distanced from the situation. In part, I suppose this was also a reaction to me. I had changed in a sense. I had adapted to coping alone, doing everything by myself in the camp and out in the bushlands while she was away — and I was still in this solitary mode when she returned.

I remember one evening in particular when we were sitting together on top of our lookout, with the bushlands all around, realising there was a tension between us. With Julie having to spend time away for family reasons, at that time and afterwards, somewhere, somehow, a void developed between us and sadly, in the year to come, it was to widen until we could no longer reach across to touch each other's hearts as we once had.

We were, of course, the greatest of

friends. Julie's support for me in the past crisis period and in the times to come was complete and helped me steer myself back on course — but I was not able to support her in the same way. My intense concern for the lions' welfare and the protection of the bushlands left me drained with very little left to give and, coupled with this, because of her absences I was without what I needed to nurture our relationship — and so our relationship was becoming a casualty of our cause.

On reflection, I feel it was astonishing that Julie had persevered for so long (over three years) with me in the bushlands. She had so often, in the emotional sense, become almost secondary to the lions and the land. At times, there was not sufficient space in my heart for both. She was living through trauma and existing in terribly harsh conditions. She endured all this first for my sake and secondly because she believed in the cause — the lions and the land. Because of her absences, I noticed the lions were becoming increasingly dis-familiar with her and had begun to regard her suspiciously. I had promoted and encouraged this throughout their rehabilitation because if wild animals are suspicious and watchful of man, distance is created from the possible dangers man can pose for them.

In the past Julie's relationship with the lions was one of mutual familiarity. Though she would be reluctant to admit to having a favourite, it was Rafiki. To her 'Squeaks' was a 'special person'. When, in the past, I had not been at the camp when the lions visited, Julie was then a kind of substitute. Of these occasions she wrote the following:

Furaha would very seldom greet me, 'Bats' would say hello with a quick head rub and then await Gareth's arrival, but 'Squeaks' would always trot up to the fence, honking, licking and head rubbing. Whenever Gareth arrived though, I would be forgotten by all three as they would rush up, crowd around him, all greeting with such excitement and fondness. I would watch this alone from inside the camp. It didn't upset me in any way — it was simply the way it was and I found it in some ways quite amusing.

Julie could have rekindled her relationship with the lions, but we decided against this as it had the risk of perhaps regressing their attitude towards people *per se*. Julie's contact with the lions became minimal and when they visited the camp, she kept out of sight of them. If the bond was not strong, the relationship would not be total and the bond was dependent upon deep mutual emotions. If total and absolute familiarity does not exist on both sides, the relationship becomes disjointed and no longer whole. Perhaps, as with the lions, this was what was happening between Julie and me too.

★ ★ ★

Not long after Julie's return to the bushlands, two incidents occurred which highlighted that this hastily put-together camp needed to be better secured. The first occurred as one morning, from the mess area, we watched the pride walking along the eastern fence. As we watched, we saw Sala, now half-grown at fourteen months, trailing behind and as she came up to a fence post, we could not believe our eyes when we realised that she was walking on our side of the fence! *Sala was inside the camp with us!* Julie quickly got into our pick-up while I opened the gate to allow her to drive out. We were deserting the camp to prevent Sala panicking when she realised that she could not reach the others. As I drove away, I left the gate open so that she could get out of the camp.

We parked about two kilometres away from camp and waited for some time, hoping that Sala had not become distressed and was finding her way out to rejoin the pride. When we drove back, I saw spoor of a lion leaving, but also spoor leading in! I instructed Julie to stay in the vehicle while I checked in the camp to make sure that none of the lions were inside. Sala, it seemed, did not find the opened gate and had been pacing beside the fence. One of the lionesses, probably Furaha, had then walked into the camp, gone to her and led her out. There was now no sign of the pride and I saw where they had headed off to the west and guessed that they were probably lying up for the day. Fortunately, a potentially volatile situation had been averted and all was now calm.

Upon entering the camp, Julie and I found where Sala had managed to enter. At the camp's far side, we found a relatively small gap in the fence and her spoor. We then wired up the gap and made a thorough check for any other parts of the fence through which the cubs could inadvertently enter the camp. I also secured the bottom of the fence and placed thorn branches on the outside against parts of the fence where the weak spots were.

The second incident was more dramatic and somewhat bizarre, occurring at sunrise only a few weeks later. At that time, Julie and I slept in separate tents. Mine was pitched close to the fence while hers was beside the shepherd's tree and the mess area at the centre of the camp. I awoke to the sound of a violent crash against the fence, then I felt a heavy blow of something literally bouncing off the side of my tent.

I was up in a flash and saw Rafiki outside the camp pacing along the fence, her eyes riveted on something behind me. I then saw near my tent the spoor of an impala and where it had smashed through a small gate I had cut into the fence. Hastily, I wired the gate so that Rafiki could not climb through. I then went to Julie's tent. As I did so, I could hear the impala trying to get through the fence in various parts of the camp. I rushed into Julie's tent, quickly woke her and before she really knew what was going on, I had led her to the safety of the inside of the vehicle where I told her to stay until I had resolved the problem of the impala inside the camp and a hungry lion trying to reach it from the outside.

As I turned away from the vehicle, I heard a distant cry of the impala. Rafiki, this signalled, had somehow caught it and was now killing it. I walked towards where she was and saw her trying to pull the impala through the fence. As she pulled powerfully, the impala became entwined in the wire and the fence groaned ominously. I felt that that section was going to collapse if I did not do something fast.

I had to take drastic action, and in a sense abscond with her kill if the situation was to be diffused. I ran and got a bucket full of water, then returned. Never would I normally have interfered when my lions were newly in possession of prey — possession in lions can elicit lightning aggression. As Rafiki saw me approaching, she strained backwards with her impala. I rushed up, shouted and threw the water at her. Poor Rafiki! She leapt back and I shouted 'No!', keeping her a few paces away.

Amazingly, as if realising what I had to do, she then calmly lay down and simply watched as I set about untangling the impala from the fencing. With her closely observing this activity, it was some time before I managed to free the dead impala. I then pulled it to one side and perhaps it was adrenalin that enabled me to hoist its forty kilo weight above my head and throw it over the fence. Rafiki then quietly stepped forward, honked a passive call to me and began pulling her prey down the hillside where she disappeared for the rest of the day.

I let out a sigh of relief. I straightened and secured the damaged fence and returned to Julie in the car. She was now fully awake and was staring at me through the windscreen, somewhat wide-eyed. When I told her what had happened, she was astonished and slightly stunned by it all as was I.

★ ★ ★

It was not very long after this incident that we were paid a visit by my good friend, Peter Senamolela. Peter was the Department of Wildlife game warden responsible for the Bobirwa area, that part of eastern Botswana which included the Tuli bushlands. He was always tremendously supportive of our work and assisted Julie with her plans to create an environmental education nature reserve and centre in the bushlands for Botswanan children. Often Julie would visit local schools with Peter to give talks and slide presentations, encouraging the establishment of wildlife clubs.

On this occasion, however, Peter had come to inform us that the President of Botswana, Sir Quett Masire, was soon to tour near the bushlands and he suggested that he try to organise an opportunity for me to give a slide presentation to the President. I told Peter that I would be privileged to have the opportunity of putting across first-hand the lions' story and our aspirations and hopes for the Tuli bushlands.

Later a message reached us that the presentation had been organised and the venue was the Zanzibar Hotel, some eighty kilometres from the reserve. When the day arrived, we set out for Zanzibar hours ahead of time in case we had problems with the vehicle (which, for once, we did not). The Zanzibar to which we were travelling was not the one of coral beaches and the aroma of cloves, but a small settlement on the banks of the Limpopo where there was water perennially in the river.

My usual bush attire is a pair of shorts and canvas shoes — certainly not suitable for a meeting with the President. Julie dug out my only pair of reasonable long trousers and a shirt while I searched high and low for a tie which I knew was somewhere in the camp. Julie borrowed a smart dress from a friend for the occasion.

After we had arrived at the hotel and set up my slide projector in the 'conference room', we changed from our bush clothes into our more presentable ones. I wore a tie, which I had eventually found, for the first time in years. Later, members of the public gathered outside the hotel to await the President and his entourage.

Just before sunset, we heard the sound of military helicopters approaching and they landed on an area of bare ground just outside the hotel. On his arrival, the President and his wife waved and smiled at the people, shaking hands with the young and old as they were warmly welcomed.

After the President had entered the hotel, our local member of parliament, James Maruatona, came up to me to finalise a few arrangements and to inform me that the President and his wife would soon be ready for the slide presentation.

We re-checked the slide projector and the seating arrangements in the conference room and soon afterwards, we were told that the Presidential entourage was on its way. Julie and I stood at the entrance and Mr Maruatona led the President and his wife into the room. The President grasped my hand firmly and said, 'Hello, Mr Big Lion' — which immediately put me at ease. I introduced the President and his wife to Julie and once he and his entourage had entered the room, the presentation began.

As I spoke, I noticed that the room was becoming increasingly crowded as members of the public came in to watch too. It became a very full house. In half an hour, I had outlined the lions' story and told several anecdotes, such as how the lions had saved my life from an attacking leopard, how both Rafiki and Furaha had led me to their newborn cubs and ended the talk with Batian's story. After the talk, the President and members of his entourage asked me questions about my work and he said that he hoped that Sala and Tana would have a good future in the bushlands and that one day they would in turn produce the next generation of the Adamson pride.

At the end of the presentation, he and his wife came up to Julie and me to thank us and we said our goodbyes. Before we left, we found Peter to thank him for organising the occasion, then headed to the hotel bar for a well-earned drink. As we entered the bar, we saw several friends including Bane Sesa, the head of Immigration for the area. We were greeted warmly, congratulated on our presentation and beers were handed to us. Sesa was astonished by my appearance — he was so used to seeing me dusty and in shorts. His eyes widened on seeing me in long trousers, clean shirt and wearing a tie. Then he chuckled heartily, affectionately slapping me on the back. I think he was very proud of me.

Later we left and began the long journey back to camp relieved that the presentation had been successful. It had been a unique opportunity of informing President Masire, in a very personal way, of the lions' story and our hopes and fears for the Tuli bushlands and its wild denizens. The President of Botswana is known traditionally as 'Tautona' which means 'The Great Lion'. Symbolically, as in so many countries and cultures worldwide, here too the lion is seen as a king and all powerful.

7

In Between Times

OVER a period of a week, with the help of Jippy from Shashe, later with Bingo from Hatari, then with staff from Charter, I hauled down much of what remained of the fencing at old Tawana and transported it in bundles to the three respective camps. As mentioned earlier, I was supplying the staff with fencing so that they could re-erect it where they were housed by the landowners, and be protected from predators which were attracted to the camps by the game congregating at the artificial waterholes. The fencing would also give them greater protection from elephants, which, in greater numbers than in previous winters, were now using the camps' waterholes.

The Pitsani and other natural seeps had all but dried up, until the only remaining natural waterpoint in my lions' range was that of 'New England'. New England, so named by white pioneers a century earlier, is a perennial spring beneath a massive fig tree just inside the boundary with the neighbouring Tuli Safari Area in Zimbabwe. This spring was to become, in the height of the drought, the only natural waterpoint in well over 200 square kilometres of that portion of the bushlands. Never in living memory had the bushlands water table become so desperately depleted. There beneath the fig tree, water bravely pumped like a tiny heart upwards from the ground, pushing tiny flecks of sand towards the surface and this pulsating spring maintained the small pools which supported literally thousands of animals.

On occasions, I would meet my friend David Mupungu near this spring. David was the hard-working warden of the Tuli Safari Area. He would take me to where the little heartbeat of the bushlands, the spring, pumped and sitting there by the mini oasis in a vast land depleted of moisture, we would discuss the situation in our respective sides of the bushlands. At that time, David had the arduous task of attempting to contain a massive invasion of livestock. Literally thousands of head of cattle, goats, donkeys and sheep were being illegally grazed in his reserve by the Shashe livestock owners. The livestock were cropping to the roots the essential winter feed of the wild animals. On our side, the annual invasion of livestock from beyond the Shashe was being successfully contained for the first time. The Government, prompted by our reports on the matter, had stepped in. The Botswana Defence Force unit, based in the bushlands, took control of the situation. First they warned Zimbabwean livestock owners that their livestock would be shot if found grazing on the Botswana side. Then, with this warning going unheeded, they shot some cows and the warning was driven home and the livestock owners kept their herds and flocks mostly on their side. David, though, being based in Zimbabwe, could not take such drastic action by killing his people's livestock — retaliation could have occurred and so he and his rangers persevered in attempting to herd the livestock out of the reserve.

It was an incredibly tough winter, but the wild animals are equally tough. Despite the conditions, very few animals were dying because of the drought. This was in stark contrast to the cattle country to the west where devastation was taking place amongst the herds. Also, unlike in the bushlands, in the game farms of the northern Transvaal, the wild animals were also perishing. Because they were contained and because fencing had carved up the ecosystem, the animals could no longer move as the seasons dictated and thus confined, they died. The Tuli animals were living within a fenceless wilderness of some two thousand square kilometres, moving even into habitat beyond this area — and so because of the relative freedom of movement and their resilience to drought, they were surviving.

I had witnessed a similar drought period ten years previously. Then there had been a massive die-off amongst the zebra and wildebeest, but I feel that this was not due only to the harsh conditions, but also to a contributory factor — disease. What I had seen then was probably a natural regulation at work. The survivors of that drought had since built up strength and in the present drought, they were remaining healthy.

In the drought of 1983, the mega-herbivores, the Tuli elephants, did not experience die-off, indicating that the population had not reached saturation in relation to habitat available to them. This again silenced in my opinion the calls for culling made by managers and some landowners in the bushlands, a conclusion they reached as a result of what they perceived to be the elephants' 'detrimental damage' to trees.

In this drought, the elephants again remained largely unaffected although a form of self-regulation beyond the norm (i.e. reduced calving rate) seemed to have been triggered. During the height of the dry time, there were twelve or so reported cases (and perhaps that number again remained unreported) of young elephants being found dead or dying. In each case, the elephants were all males of the same age found alone. There was no obvious reason as to why this was occurring. My conclusion was that Nature was prompting a small specific category of the Tuli elephant population to die. Perhaps in a response to the conditions, the family cows were driving away these young bulls at an unusually young age. This normally occurs once the bulls have reached adolescence. It is possible that by being driven away so young, the bulls could not emotionally, as social animals, or to a lesser extent, physically cope with being alone and fending for themselves.

I found several of these youngsters dead and one, as it was dying. On a rise of sandstone, I came upon a young bull lying on its side, seemingly unable to right itself. It was an awful sight. The sun beat down upon him and heat radiated upwards from the baking rock. He was being saturated in a fierce heat. I watched him draw water from his stomach with his trunk and attempt to splash it upon his head and ears. I rushed away to bring water and returned to pour it over him, trying desperately to give him relief as he died. His eyes seemed like those of another being trapped within a dying body. They were alert and peered out in fear of me — man. On seeing his fear,

I kept out of his vision and hoped the water was easing the pain of his death.

A friend of mine had set out from a camp to destroy the young bull and, knowing this, I left just before he arrived, selfishly not wanting to witness any more of the suffering. In the short time between my leaving and my friend arriving, the bull passed away. I had witnessed few of his last moments of life. Even though his death was natural and not inflicted by man, it was to me a death of greater magnitude than other deaths by natural causes I had witnessed in the bushlands. What I mean by this may not sound logical, but an elephant's death to me is like a breath of wilderness being stilled. The whole lives on, but a small portion is deadened. Recognising an elephant's intelligence, its human animal qualities, the death of an elephant causes me to react similarly as to the death of a friend, or of a brother perhaps.

★ ★ ★

It was during this time of dryness and death of the young bulls that we were

153

visited by author and environmental journalist, Brian Jackman. Brian's writings had been an influence on me five years previously when I began to write my first book, *Cry for the Lions*. I had read and greatly enjoyed his book, *The Marsh Lions*, in which he described so completely the life of lion prides and the life around them. In words, he achieved what some writers in Africa do not. He captured the soul of the wilderness. Brian is a lion fanatic and like me, was imbued with their personality and spirit. He had written to Julie and me some time earlier saying that he was due to visit one of the game lodges in the bushlands and asked whether he could visit us. We replied that it would be our pleasure and that I had wanted to meet him for a long time.

Brian was also a friend of George Adamson and had visited him at Kora many times to document portions of George's twilight years for international newspapers and magazines. I knew George, somewhere, would be pleased that Brian was to see how his work had not died with him, and that the freedom and the philosophy lived on.

For three days, I introduced Brian to the bushlands, an area which he quickly took to. Each night at camp, we would listen expectantly for the lions, but each night, they could neither be heard nor did they appear and although he did not visibly show it, I knew that Brian was disappointed. On the morning that Brian was due to depart, a magical occurrence took place which I think Brian's own words best describe. The following is the opening of an article he wrote after his visit. It was entitled 'Last of the Free'.

The cry of the young Englishman carried in the cool air of a Botswana winter's dawn. 'Come on Rafiki, Come on Furaha.' Again, he cupped his hands to his lips and called, his voice echoing among the stony hills. Silence. And then, from a kilometre off, the answering roar of a lion. His face broke into a grin of pure delight. 'They're coming,' he said.

Suddenly, impala began to snort in alarm. Gareth Patterson gestured at me to keep out of sight, afraid that my presence would scare the lions away, then opened the gate of his camp compound and stepped outside.

Moments later, Rafiki appeared, a full-grown lioness in her prime. I could hear the thud of her feet as she ran straight at Patterson, then rose on her hind legs to place her huge front paws over his shoulders, while he in turn hugged and stroked her tawny flanks. 'Rafiki,' he murmured and the big lioness grunted with pleasure at seeing her friend again.

Twelve years ago, I had watched George Adamson, the grand old lion man of Africa, being greeted in exactly the same way when he introduced me to his wild pride at Kora in northern Kenya. It was a sight I never expected to see again, yet here I was in Botswana, watching the man who had so modestly assumed the Adamson mantle.

It was a wonderful sight for Brian to have witnessed, seeing again the pure love between a man and a lion. Twelve years previously, he had written the following to describe what he had seen while with George:

At the sound of George Adamson's voice, the big lioness left the waterbuck kill and padded down the track towards us. 'Arusha, old girl,' Adamson cried and flung his arms around her neck.

It was an unbelievable sight! The old man smiling, the lioness resting her huge head on his shoulder, grunting her pleasure at seeing him again, and all around us, the watchful yellow eyes of Arusha's wild pride.

* * *

Brian was one of our very rare visitors. I had instilled a necessary suspicion of man in the lions and therefore did not want to retard this by having many visitors as at any time, the lions might appear and see them. I only allowed people to stay who were close to us and/or could publicise and promote the lions' cause.

As I have previously mentioned, camp life was becoming increasingly difficult for Julie as the lions had become less familiar with her due to lack of contact. Whenever they now visited me, just as I had done with Brian, I had to keep Julie as much as possible out of sight of them. They were totally wild lions, only familiar with me, but then were they not seeing me as a lion rather than as a human? They were familiar with people *per se* when their rehabilitation began and soon afterwards when work on a documentary on our lives with them commenced.

To digress a little, this documentary took almost three years to complete, but 'Born to be Free', as it was entitled, became a valuable documentation of the work and was subsequently shown in twenty-five countries around the world.

The man who directed and filmed much of the documentary in the early stages was Rick Lomba, a well-known and respected environmentalist and film-maker. Rick spent a lot of time with Julie and me at Tawana. Botswana was a country well known to Rick and a country close to his heart. He tackled environmental issues head-on, backing up his effective lobbying with hard fact.

Rick, both before and after his time with us, lobbied tirelessly in the USA and Europe against the damaging effect of Botswana's cattle industry — an industry heavily subsidised by the EEC — and against misguided donor development policies within the country. He also illustrated the environmental problem areas in his international blockbuster documentary, 'End of Eden', and went on to launch an international campaign to stop the dredging of the Okavango Delta, working closely with Greenpeace.

The initial work on the documentary on us became complicated because I decided that it would be unwise for Rick to accompany me to film me with the lions in the bush (which had been the original plan) despite their being, at that stage, still familiar with people. I felt that as they did not know him as they did me, and as he was not fully acquainted either with the vocal or body language of lions, an accident could well occur. Even though he knew that this would compromise the film he had in mind, Rick respected my decision and we worked in other ways to capture my life amongst the lions in the wilds.

On his next visit, Rick brought up a small but high quality camera and instructed me on its use so that I could film the lions interacting in the wilds. With practice, in the weeks to come, I did manage to capture some beautiful scenes that were cut into the final version of the documentary. It was a frustrating film for Rick to make as at times he would arrive at camp after travelling over 500 kms from his home, only to spend days with us without any lions for us to film. Their wanderings sometimes took them deep into the Tuli Safari Area in Zimbabwe where we could not go in search of them.

The film was completed by a separate crew, just after Brian Jackman's visit. In an intensive period of two weeks, as we had at times experienced with Rick, we did not see the lions once and had to concentrate on the other facets of our life in the bushlands, such as populations of other wild animals, the cattle issue, poaching and the drought. A few days after the crew had left the bushlands, somewhat predictably, Rafiki appeared at our camp. Julie rushed to pass on a message to the film crew and the following day, the cameraman was back in the bushlands. That afternoon, filming from our vehicle, he captured beautiful scenes of Rafiki and me together, she greeting me, us together while she ate from a kill, and she and I walking towards the lowering sun and away into the haze of the bushlands. After three long years, the final scene had been captured and it was over.

Although he was not responsible for the final version of the documentary, I will always think of the film as Rick's. Tragically, just as I was preparing to write this book and just after Rick and I had worked on a short segment for a separate documentary dealing with the return of big cats to the wilds, he was killed.

Rick was in Angola filming the courageous airlifting of animals from terrible zoo conditions in Luanda to far better conditions in South Africa. Somehow, an emaciated tiger escaped during the operation and Rick was seized by it and killed. Wild Africa lost one of its most resourceful allies and champions.

★　★　★

On the day of the first anniversary of Batian's death, I walked from 'new' Tawana down to where I had buried him beneath the cairn of stones. For the past year, I would go there twice or three times a month. Always, while walking to the cairn, I would reflect on the past and later, when leaving, I would look positively to the future. While sitting beneath the two trees near the grave, a tear or two would be shed, but the visits always left me strengthened. I drew courage from my much-loved lion.

On the day of the anniversary, I put my hand inside the hole in one of the two trees. After Batian's death, I had placed his identification collar there. To my surprise, I discovered that the hole was empty and I wondered what could have happened to the collar. I then searched thoroughly all around the grave and in the nearby mopane grove, but there was no sign of the collar. I thought that perhaps an elephant with a searching trunk had smelt it, pulled it out and dropped it nearby. Extraordinarily, I was to see his collar again — exactly a year later to the day. I found it lying just metres away from his grave near the spoor of a young male lion, and of this mystery I will tell later in the story.

I walked away, wondering about the missing collar, but later, as I was approaching camp, my thoughts turned to the present and to the future. Rafiki and Furaha were now four years old, two magnificent and healthy lionesses and just a month before, Sala and Tana had turned one year old. They were now almost half grown with Sala slightly taller and stockier than Tana.

Strangely, I had been noticing Rafiki spending time away from the rest of the pride and this was to increase in the months ahead. I suspected that she was coming into oestrus and was wandering in search of a male. Normally, a lioness with cubs will not breed again until her young are emerging into sub-adulthood, at about sixteen to eighteen months, when they are no longer dependent upon her.

Sala was not this age, but Rafiki seemed at that time to hand the responsibility of her over to Furaha.

Late that night, I became aware of the soft cooing of a lion. I rose, replied with the 'whoo who' answering call and as I stepped out of the tent, I saw Rafiki in the light of my torch. Perhaps she had sensed my mixed emotions of that time, the anniversary of Batian's death, and had come to be near me. We sat together for some time before she rose, stretched, and rubbed her head against me for one last time before walking away into the night.

The following morning, well after sunrise, she re-appeared and indicated that she wished me to follow her, which I did. She led me to the eastern edge of the high ground, then downwards. I suspected she had made a kill. Presuming the rest of the pride might be nearby and not wanting to startle the cubs with my sudden appearance, I returned to camp. What transpired was that Rafiki, alone, had killed a sub-adult eland and the rest of the pride only joined her the following day after they had first visited me, appearing from the west. So, at the time of their fourth year, Rafiki, Furaha and the cubs were together, feasting well and they were content. So was I.

The next evening, the pride came to me. Julie was away again and I sat amongst them as a spirit of contentment and calm pervaded. Sala came within three paces of me. She was always the bolder of the two youngsters, always wishing to get close to me. She approached, then lay down and eventually slept. The cubs would never have the relationship of total trust I shared with their mothers and I would never initiate contact, letting them come to me only if they wished. The closeness shared with Sala that evening would never occur during daylight when they were much more shy and would keep a distance. Only at night would they rest up nearby as I sat with their mothers.

After darkness descended, I quietly rose and returned to camp. Later, when I went to my tent to sleep, I heard their contented sighs as they rested up only twenty metres away. The leisurely sighs of resting, full-bellied, contented lions is to me the most relaxing sound in the world and soon I too was asleep. The following morning, they were gone with their spoor heading west. I followed for a kilometre or so, then saw Rafiki's spoor splitting away from that of the pride and heading north. Seeing this, I thought once again, 'Yes, she's seeking a mate.'

I did not see any of the lions until over a week later when I arrived at camp after collecting Julie on her return to the bushlands. My meeting with them that evening was unusual. We drove into the camp and as we did so, I spotted lion spoor beside the fence. I went out to investigate and as I followed the spoor, I began to think I was imagining things as there seemed to be the spoor of not four lions, but five! The ground was very hard and therefore the spoor was not clear. The fifth spoor seemed larger though — almost like Batian's. I concentrated so much on trying to decipher the tracks that I unknowingly walked past where Furaha was lying with her cubs. Only her characteristic low 'Aaoow' alerted me to their presence. With surprise, I looked up and with equal surprise saw just the three of them — no sign of Rafiki, nor of the mysterious fifth lion.

I remained standing there as Furaha rose, yawning as she stretched and arched her back before padding towards me. We greeted each other, then together walked back towards the camp with the cubs trailing behind us. At camp, they drank water and lay up peacefully on the hill's edge. Julie, sitting out of sight of the pride, was pleased to have the lions nearby on her return, and as the sun set, we chatted softly, catching up with each other's news. A little later, I told her how I was reasonably sure I had seen the spoor of two other lions out beyond the camp.

As we were discussing this, we suddenly heard the cubs' very nasal, 'whoa, whou, whou' grunts — a sound they would make if startled or frightened. We turned our heads and briefly saw them dashing below the hillside. Then we heard Rafiki cooing and, rising to go to the fence to greet her, I could not understand why the cubs had reacted as they had. Was there in fact another lion nearby, aside from Rafiki?

As I bent down to fondly greet her and as she was pushing her body against mine, I suddenly froze. Not thirty metres away, backlit by the setting sun, I saw the head and shoulders of a beautiful young male lion. He was lying facing me, partially concealed by the grass and low mopane branches. This was my first meeting with Nelion.

I slowly stood upright, then backed away as surely he could see me and therefore would intuitively fear me as man. To my utter surprise, he showed no fear and just watched me with an open-faced, totally non-aggressive stare. He was an exceptionally handsome lion and I was somewhat shaken by his facial similarity to Batian. I walked back, now in a daze, to where Julie was hidden from the lions' view in the mess area. I recounted to her what had happened, telling her too that it was as if Batian were out there.

Later that night, when I was in my tent, I heard loud lapping sounds from the water drum. I shone my torch and saw, a few yards away, the young male drinking. After he had drunk, I stepped quietly out of my tent and crossed to Julie's. I wanted her to see him too. Standing near her tent, I shone the torch again towards the fence and there he was — I half expected him not to have a tail, his similarity to Batian was so striking. His calm behaviour was also extraordinary. My lionesses' past suitors, the Zimmale brothers, had always acted aggressively towards me. Once, when I had come across one of the Zimmales mating with Rafiki, he had attacked and almost leapt into my open jeep as Julie and I attempted to get away.

This young male was so peaceful, and had no reason to be. Lions normally react with fear and, at times, aggression when confronted with man on foot, although generally in tourist areas, they are not too perturbed by people in vehicles. This is because they become accustomed to the man/vehicle combination, but exceedingly rarely do they become used to the sight of man on foot.

I named him Nelion, as this was the name of M'Batian's brother. They were two celebrated Masaai brothers, two *laibons* (clairvoyants) and chieftains who lived a hundred years ago in Kenya. Their names were given to the twin peaks of Mount Kenya which tower above the land where, four years earlier, my lions had been born.

That night, I thought about Nelion and his relationship with my pride. Although the cubs had obviously been startled by his appearance, I do feel Furaha had previously been acquainted with him. Otherwise pandemonium would have occurred. On his appearance, Furaha had let out a short half-hearted whine of warning, but did not move from where she lay. I felt therefore that Nelion was not a threat to the cubs (it was always my great fear that a potential new pride male might kill them). I wondered whether this calm young male was going to peacefully take Batian's place as pride male. I was to see more of this young prince in the weeks ahead.

* * *

My pride was now, and had been for over two years, removed from the world of man in which they had grown up

170

after the death of their mother when just days old. The rehabilitation initiated by George at Kora and completed by me in the Tuli bushlands had, against great odds, been a success and now the new generation of Adamson lions, Sala and Tana, were heading towards sub-adulthood.

However, the pride was not always left undisturbed in the bushlands and in the past two years had probably been viewed from the game drive vehicles by several hundred tourists. Almost all the tourists who saw my pride would have been totally unaware of their background, not knowing that they had been reared and successfully released back into the wilds by man. Because of my conservation watchdog presence and perhaps also because of professional jealousy, I learnt that the game guides of one particular safari company had been instructed by management not to tell the tourists of the pride's fascinating history. A ridiculous policy as the tourists' bush experience would have been enhanced by the lions' story. Photographs of Batian, Rafiki and Furaha probably exist in photo albums throughout the world and, sadly, these tourists are unaware of the special lions they had seen hunting, lazing and playing while in the bushlands.

Before the birth of the cubs and the death of Batian, very occasionally I, with the trio, was spotted by tourists on game drives. To watch the human response on seeing us, and feeling what it must be like to be viewed from the lions' perspective, was fascinating. For example, one winter's morning, after attempting a hunt with the lions, we stopped to rest in a fairly open area and lay together, soaking up the sun's rays. (Early winter mornings in the bushlands can be bitterly cold.) I was lost in thought when suddenly I heard a vehicle below us. My first instinct for some reason was to move away. The vehicle, though not in sight, was near and its occupants might see me dashing away. I had no option but to stay where I was with the lions. I realised that the vehicle would pass within 150 metres of us and the lions lifted their heads to stare in its direction as it approached.

Neither the tourists nor the guide saw

Batian, July 1988 - July 1991
(Louise Gubb)

Right:
Julie during happier times at the old Tawana Camp

Below: Sticks

Above: "I was patrolling an area of some 80km alone"

Below: "I cursed myself for walking in and upsetting the Shashe lionesses"

Above: Drought. "In past years water could always be found, now all that could be seen was a baked depression"

Below: "In this drought the elephants again remained largely unaffected"

Above: End of another Tuli lion: lured into and shot on a South African border farm

Below: Lion skull. "For years lions have been destroyed for moving out to prey upon cattle"

Above: Furaha, as a young lioness, two years before she died

Below: "Were Furaha, Sala and Tana killed for a crime they did not commit?"

Last days together – Gareth and Furaha

Left: "I now spent long periods alone in the bushlands"
(Sue Usher)

Right: "Is this my souls land, or just soil to cover my bones?"

us initially, but as they were about to pass by, I clearly heard the yell of 'Lion!', then 'Man!'. The vehicle came to a standstill, then, almost stalling, lurched away. It was that safari company's policy also not to stop if guides came across me with the lions in the wild. I heard the tourists calling, 'Stop! Stop!', but the guide (probably very reluctantly) had to heed company policy and drove on. My face broke into a broad grin as I saw the tourists climbing into the open vehicle's back seats for a last fleeting view of the most unexpected sight. Soon they were out of view and my lions laid their heads down again with a sigh.

On another occasion, my lions and I were chasing a porcupine when, unexpectedly, a vehicle from the same safari company appeared. On hearing it, I thought I had time to dash out of sight, but later learnt that I had not gone undetected. The tourists had seen me first with the lions, then dashing away. I also learnt that when they arrived back at the game lodge after the morning's drive, they enquired of the management as to the identity of this person with the lions.

Again, keeping to 'company policy', they were informed that they must have seen a 'poacher'. Bloody strange poacher who roams around with three lions! The person who gave this reply must have thought his guests extremely gullible. On a serious note, however, I did think it was sad that tourists in such situations could not be allowed to know the truth and in turn share a small portion of the magic of my relationship with the lions.

On another occasion, I was spotted from a game drive vehicle, not from the safari company. The game ranger driving was my friend, David Marupane, and some of his guests were people known to me. I was lying on the ground with the lions under a shepherd's tree on the banks of the Pitsani river sixty metres away from a bush track. I heard the vehicle, then saw it appear from along the riverine bush. Then again, there was the shout, 'Lion!', whereupon David instantly stopped the vehicle. Then I heard, somewhat more faint, the words ' . . . can't believe it . . . a man!' I then heard David saying to his guest, 'Yes, it's Gareth with his lions.' I stayed completely still as binoculars and cameras were raised. I was in the lions' world, with them as one of them. I could not stand and wave or anything like that. After five minutes or so, David started his vehicle and drove away. As he did so, I saw him turn his head and his white teeth gleamed as we exchanged knowing, if not mischievous, smiles and I gave him a little wave. When, back in the world of man, we next met, we had a hearty chuckle about the whole thing with David imitating some of his guests' reactions on seeing me and the lions.

The lions, mine and others, were not always approached and viewed in a sensible way by people driving in the bushlands. The majority of the game guides were old friends and they would never harass lions. They knew lion behaviour well and respected them. This was not always the case with people from the private non-commercial camps where city people, the landowners or their friends, might drive themselves around the bushlands without an experienced game ranger — and the following tale illustrates the lack of sensitivity or respect for lions sometimes shown.

One public holiday period, when the reserve was filled with landowners and their families and friends, my pride brought down and killed a massive eland bull. The following morning, people in a game drive vehicle spotted my lions and radioed to others where the lions were. Soon, vehicles were coming in from all directions to view them. My lions moved away from their kill and hid about one hundred metres away in thick bush along a stream bank.

At about midday, yet another vehicle appeared, this time with children as well as adults on board. Then the most irresponsible thing happened. Although well knowing that the lions were nearby, the people got off the vehicle and walked up to the dead eland. I am amazed that my lions did not charge at the people in defence not only of their cubs, but also their kill. Fortunately, the pride, undoubtedly looking at the people, remained hidden. The irresponsibility could so easily have led to an explosive situation and resulted in the scattering of adults and children — or worse.

The evening game drive vehicles again congregated at the lions' kill site — some arriving with drunken occupants at well past eleven o'clock that night. The following morning, the traffic began once again and finally my lions could bear it no longer. The people saw my pride trotting away, and nervously looking over their backs as they deserted their well-earned kill. During the day, with the kill unprotected by the pride, the vultures descended and fed, and at nightfall, the hyaenas gathered for the feast.

Late in the afternoon, my four appeared at my camp and seemed nervous. Also, they were not full from eating as the disturbance meant they had not been able to feed as they normally would have. At sunset, I once again sat with them upon the hill's edge. Here no vehicles would disturb them and soon our usual group calm descended. As it darkened, I saw across the bushlands the flicker of lights — the game drive vehicles' lights and their spotlights, flickering like fireflies as their occupants searched for lions. Tonight the lions were again at peace and away from the irritation of noisy vehicles, noisy people and blinding lights.

It was not long after they had had to desert a kill that I witnessed how the 'cubs' were now taking on adult responsibilities. One morning, I awoke to the sounds of lions drinking from the water drum outside the camp. I got up and saw it was Rafiki and Furaha. They were incredibly thirsty and had bloodied faces indicating that they had recently killed.

I also noticed that Sala and Tana were not with them which was very strange and a little worrying. I became increasingly concerned when Furaha and Rafiki began to roar loudly, their voices being heard by all for miles around. I feared that, on making a kill, they had had a clash with Zimmale and had been separated from the cubs — or that worse had occurred.

After drinking, Furaha and Rafiki began heading off in the opposite direction into which they had roared. I decided to go with them to discover what indeed was going on. We headed south to that lovely lonely land of no roads or camps between the high ground and the Pitsani.

After walking for three quarters of an hour, both lionesses became watchful, pausing at times to listen and stare around. All I knew was that we were approaching some situation or other. We walked parallel to what I called Artillery Hill. (On the hilltop, I had discovered long-forgotten battlements built a hundred years earlier during the Boer War.) The lionesses stopped suddenly, seeing what I could not. They then called their 'Oowhey oowhey' — 'Where are you?' — call, to which there was a reply in front of us. They trotted ahead and as I moved too, I saw a kill, a large wildebeest bull.

It was being guarded by Sala and Tana and they had kept away the persistent jackals and a nearby hyaena which loped away at speed upon seeing me. Man was not meant to be part of the kill scene for him!

A greeting between the lions took place before Furaha, Tana and Sala climbed up to the top of Artillery Hill. There, high up under a shepherd's tree they could see all around the land that was theirs. Rafiki took over guard duty of the kill, eating a little before lying up and allowing me to slice off some meat to take back to camp.

From what I had witnessed I realised Sala and Tana were undertaking certain adult responsibilities. I was proud and knew that now they had reached this stage, the pride was strengthened.

8

Projects for Protection

IN the first week of August 1992, Julie and I had planned to leave the bushlands for a week of complete rest. We were exhausted and in three years had never left the area to take a holiday together. The night before we had prepared to leave; we excitedly packed our clothes, tidied the camp, made sure that there was a lot of water in the lions' drinking drums and chatted about how much good the rest would do us. Privately I hoped that the break would help close the void developing between us.

The following morning, we drove out of the camp in our battered pick-up, but we had gone no more than five kilometres when we developed a change of heart. Could we actually afford the holiday financially? Would the pick-up really get us to where we were planning to go?

What about the lack of anti-poaching work taking place? The questions caused us to decide not to leave. We drove on to the small town of Alldays, across the border, where we bought supplies. In a pathetic attempt to compensate for not going away, we decided to splash out and buy some frozen fish and I bought Julie some chocolate bars which she so enjoyed. Then we returned to new Tawana, and laughed at the ridiculousness of the situation. I told Julie that at least we had enjoyed the anticipation of going away on holiday.

Any money we had, or I gained through book royalties, went straight back into the costs of our work. We had not earned salaries over the past three years and now were surviving on a shoestring budget. We could hardly keep ourselves going, but at the same time, had to strive towards fulfilling our objectives of a holistic full protection of the Tuli bushlands and its wild inhabitants.

We attempted to raise money in traditional ways, but encountered prejudices; some claimed that our work did not have scientific credibility or that 'lions are not endangered'. I dispute both points, both then and now. Firstly, with the rehabilitation of the lions, the knowledge I gained, the processes I recognised, coupled with what Joy and George documented can form the basis of what will become an increasingly necessary tool in big cat conservation. Secondly, as to lions not being recognised as 'endangered' at that time, I am thankful that such thinking is changing, albeit somewhat late. We produced proposals for various projects and always, at the last moment, hopes for funding were dashed. From time to time, we felt that we could no longer even keep ourselves going.

At these times, almost as if telepathy were at work, we would, out of the blue, receive a cheque which would tide us over. Two top advertising men, John Hunt and Reg Lascaris, were members of a safari syndicate in the Tuli and deeply appreciated the spiritual value of the wilderness. We shall always be indebted to John and Reg for making the difference.

Battling to cover our own costs frustrated us as we too needed the big funding for essential large projects. One of these projects was for what we called the 'Batian Fence'. For years, Tuli lions had been lured into neighbouring South African game farms and shot on baits, just as Batian had been. In the past, between 1983 and 1986, as a young game ranger working on one of the larger private reserves, I had urged the authorities to establish a predator-deterrent fence between ourselves and the South African farms. Sadly, no action was taken. After I left the area in 1986, ironically, the actions of the South African government to prevent incursion by freedom fighters from Zimbabwe and Botswana assisted the lions. The government erected a huge electrified fence system along the Limpopo which covered much of our boundary with the farms beyond. Unfortunately, however, for an unknown reason, a 37–kilometre stretch remained unfenced and it was here that Batian and other lions past and present were lured out.

The following is an extract from the introduction of my first book and is an account of how three Tuli lions

I had named the Silver Manes were lured by tape sounds and baits and how they died:

The lions covered about four kilometres in the fading light before they heard the sounds (taped hyaena and jackal feeding calls). Never before, though, had these lions heard the sounds coming from the south, across and beyond the dry riverbed of the Limpopo, where man was prolific and wild game scarce. They moved towards the sounds which suddenly and unnaturally ceased before beginning again, louder than before, and urging the lions to a meal.

Upon reaching the riverbed, the lions slid down the bank, trotted across the sugary sand and up the opposite side where they were confronted with a farmer's fence. They scrambled below the wire and entered a great open area of ploughed land. The feeding sounds had become louder and as darkness set in, the lions could hear the occasional noise of human voices. In the gloom, a vehicle was visible, but this did not break their stride as they moved closer to the hyaena calls. These lions had never associated vehicles with death or danger. When, as tiny cubs, the blur had cleared from their eyes, (tourist) vehicles had been one of their first sights. Never in their lives had they been chased or harassed by vehicles.

The pungent smell of rumen content hung in the air like a warm wet cloth. It soon led them to a carcass, a freshly killed and skinned goat, and a total absence of hyaena. Upon reaching the carcass, they typically began to swipe at each other, growling and snarling, as the feeding started. As they fed, a metallic click came from the vehicle and a light illuminated the feeding lions. They paused momentarily before recommencing feeding as they knew that the carcass would soon be consumed.

A shot, then another, erupted from the nearby vehicle. One lion spun into the air, its back injured, and on hitting the ground, it pathetically attempted to crawl out of the circle of light and away from death. Another, mortally wounded, with blood spurting from its throat, tried to flee when another bullet smacked wetly into its belly. It bellowed in pain as the third lion, as yet unscathed, bounded away. Two more shots were fired at the fleeing lion and one hit its front right leg and the other its back. The lion cartwheeled in the air and slammed into the broken soil, twitching spasmodically.

All three lions lay in an obscene triangle of destruction, barely alive, as blood seeped from their bodies. The innocent young males had been lured by tape recordings, a loudspeaker and a bait, to be condemned to death for the pleasure of the farmer and his friends. As the vehicle was driven towards one of the wounded victims, the lion snarled and a khaki-clad figure quickly despatched a bullet into the lion's head. Like many of his kind before him, this young lion's final vision had been of man. All three lions had been condemned to the same violent end of terror and pain. A little later, their limp bodies were unceremoniously bundled into another vehicle and taken to the farmhouse . . .

After the death of Batian and other lions, I knew that we could wait no longer, or even expect others with the financial means to act on our recommendations. We now had to somehow find the support and funding ourselves, even though we could scarcely keep ourselves going with food and fuel for the vehicle.

I initiated meetings with members of the South African Veterinary Department whose responsibility was an electrified veterinary fence along the 37-kilometre stretch — a fence that would largely prevent elephants crossing into South Africa, but was inadequate to deter lions. Dr Loocks of the Veterinary Department was sympathetic to the situation and soon we had approval by his department for the lion-deterrent fencing, which would consist of two electrified strands being attached to the existing fence just above ground level. Lions are notorious for crawling beneath fences as opposed to climbing over them and it is extraordinary how little space they require to do so. A lion, about to crawl beneath the fence, would come into contact with the offset electric strands, and would receive a sharp shock, which would deter him from crossing.

Dr Loocks' department then came forward, undertaking to erect and maintain on an ongoing basis the deterrent fence providing the materials, such as solar panels, energisers and wire. This was a marvellous gesture. If monies were generated, the prevention of lions being lured to their deaths could at last become a reality.

We then excitedly sent a proposal and budget to the Landowners' Association, as well as individuals and organisations. Our high hopes were gradually lowered as time passed. The money required for the deterrent system was just under R20,000 — approximately £3,500 sterling. I tried to encourage donations by pledging R3,000, half of my entire savings which we could not afford, in the hope that it would motivate others. The response was minimal. Depressingly, the project became less and less of a reality.

When approached by us for funding for similar projects, a representative of one conservation organisation had commented (quite rightly, I think) that public money could not be used for a project on land owned privately by wealthy South African landowners — and that it was the responsibility of the landowners, not the public, to afford protection to wild animals on their land.

As I write today, two years later, the need for a predator-deterrent fence is ironically almost unnecessary. This is because of a wonderful development initiative — the Peace Park initiative to transform the South African border farms into a conservation area. When this comes about, lions will be free and safe to cross the Limpopo into South Africa. So there need not be any more losses, like that of Batian, the Silver Manes, and so many other lions who lost their lives in those lands in the past.

In time, prides may form and reside here, living out their lives where previously their kind would only last hours or a few days before fatally meeting man and his guns. However, it is still essential for there to be predator-proof fencing on the western boundary of the bushlands bordering the livestock areas.

★ ★ ★

Another project on which we worked hard was that of environmental education. Initially, we would visit schools and give slide presentations to the children on the lions' story. In time, Julie became the area co-ordinator for the Association of Wildlife Clubs of Botswana, a constantly growing association whose main aim is to promote, through the establishment of clubs in schools and colleges, a greater understanding of the need and importance of conserving wildlife in Botswana. When Julie became the area co-ordinator, the Association of Wildlife Clubs had approximately 4000 club members countrywide.

Members of wildlife clubs would undertake in their immediate communities various environmental activities such as tree planting, litter collection and bee-keeping, with the highlight of the year being the opportunity to undertake field trips to some of Botswana's famous game reserves, such as Chobe. These field trips were essential as they gave young people, often for the very first time, the opportunity to see large wild animals such as elephants and buffaloes. On such field trips in the National Parks, the Wildlife Club might assist wardens by, for example, digging trenches for piping to provide alternative water sources for wildlife.

Unfortunately, in Julie's area, Eastern Botswana, where the country is most populated, the Wildlife Clubs had little access to wilderness areas since the northern reserves, such as Chobe, were inaccessible due to their vast distance away from our area. To address the children's important need for field trips, Julie began to seek permission from the Landowners' Association to bring groups of children into the Tuli bushlands on field trips. Sadly, the Landowners' Association viewed the proposal negatively.

It was a 'catch 22' scenario. The Tuli bushlands is privately owned and not a gazetted government conservation area, but the wildlife inhabiting the bushlands, like all wildlife in Botswana, is state owned, belonging to the nation. However, children were being denied access to view their natural heritage due to the ownership of land. This was immensely frustrating. At times, we would receive a radio call informing us that a bus filled with children had unexpectedly arrived at the border post hoping to meet up with us and wishing to view the bushlands' wildlife. On these not infrequent occasions, we would drop whatever we were doing and drive for an hour and a quarter to the border to meet the expectant children and their teachers.

We would then have to embarrassingly tell the group that because the area was privately owned and not a national park, we could not guide them around the bushlands. At times, to make things worse, it was mistakenly understood that Julie and I were in fact landowners and that we were denying them the opportunity of seeing animals.

Some of the Wildlife Club groups may have travelled over two hundred kilometres to the bushlands and on hearing of the situation from us, their tremendous disappointment was under-standable. This would wrench our hearts.

Normally, in a small attempt to compensate, I would give the group a talk on my work with the lions. Gaborone, one of our immigration official friends, would also assist by first telling the children a little of the history of the area, showing the children the Limpopo river and explaining how when it flows strongly, tourists enter the country by crossing the river in the cable car which is strung across from the South African side to our side.

After this, we would lead the group to a huge mashatu tree on the river bank and there I would give a talk. The children were fascinated by the lions' story and would always ask a host of questions about my relationship with the lions. After the talk and question time, sadly the Wildlife Club group would have to depart homewards without even seeing a single elephant.

It was a sorry situation and Julie became even more determined to address the children's important need to view wildlife in the Tuli bushlands. She gained, in time, the approval of a syndicate of landowners to bring children on to a reserve in the extreme north-west of the bushlands for environmental awareness weekends. Before this could be developed, our local Member of Parliament, Mr James Maruatona, took our idea further and suggested that, with the Association of Wildlife Clubs and the Department of Wildlife & National Parks, we undertake the feasibility of establishing a nature reserve for Wildlife Clubs.

Plans to create a community benefiting environmental education reserve on tribal land bordering the Tuli bushlands developed. The long-term goal was that this game reserve would eventually, by the dropping of fencing, become incorporated into the total Tuli bushlands. Julie worked hard towards this and, with game warden

Peter Senamolela, held meetings with members of the local communities, local chiefs and representatives of the Land Board. The project was greeted with much enthusiasm. When we reached this stage of consensus, James Maruatona sent his own representatives into the communities to discuss the proposed reserve, and he too talked about it at public meetings while on official tours. He also asked me to write up a detailed proposal on the proposed reserve — he would arm himself with its contents when pushing for approval in Parliament.

At the time of writing, this is the stage we have reached and hopefully, with final approval and donor funding, Tswana children and adults in Eastern Botswana will have free access to a portion of wilderness in which they can learn about and promote conservation — a wilderness that will be 'their' game reserve.

★ ★ ★

Late in September, we had two more visitors to the new Tawana. Professional photographer, Horst Klemm, had contacted me asking if he and his wife, Anne, could spend time with us in the bushlands. He wished to include a section on the lions in what was to become his acclaimed book, *An African Journal*. Horst and Anne spent several days with us and returned to their home in South Africa with the material they needed.

Horst's primary objective was to capture my relationship with the lions. I had agreed to this, but told him that under no circumstances should he allow himself to be seen by the lions. We designed a photograph 'hide' using my jeep from which he could watch and photograph. I stressed to Horst that my pride was to be respected as any other wild pride and that he should not be misled by the sight of me amongst them. He should not see me as a man with tame lions, but should see us as beings bonded by love and recognise that the interactions and greetings were those of the lions' world.

Furaha and her cubs appeared once while Horst and Anne were with us. Rafiki was again away with Nelion, far from the pride. On the first day of Horst's visit, we completed the photographic hide, positioning the jeep facing the direction from which I felt the lions would approach the camp. With this prepared, Horst set up his cameras and, now hidden, he waited to photograph the pride when they approached me.

With the sun low in the sky and knowing the pride was nearby, I called softly for the lions. In the east, I heard a reply, then saw Furaha followed by the cubs. After coming up to me, we greeted affectionately while the cubs looked on, and later I sat with her until the light had all but gone. After sunset, she and the youngsters drifted off towards the west. I returned to camp and Horst climbed out of the jeep.

He had taken over a hundred photographs of Furaha and me. The final shots as the sunset flamed the land were the last ever to be taken of her and me together.

Darkness was now once again to dawn.

9

The Darkness Called Death

THE nightmare began on a drizzly grey morning late in October 1992. The day before, Rafiki had appeared at camp and she was alone. During our greetings, I saw that one of her eyes was injured and later, I had driven to the border to contact and ask the advice of Andrew, the vet.

On my return, I found Rafiki below the camp's hill, upon an eland kill. Despite her eye injury (which Andrew had assured me would heal), she had alone pulled down the huge animal and I was pleased. That night, Julie and I had gone to sleep content that she was nearby. We did not know the exact whereabouts of Furaha, Sala and Tana, but suspected from the latest signs that they were north in the Tuli Safari Area.

Before continuing, I must digress and tell of the following for it has a bearing on what was to transpire on that grey morning late in October. Two weeks previously at Pont Drift, I had had a conversation with the General Manager of a tourism operation in the Tuli bushlands. The manager told me how a pride of lions, fitting the description of my lions, had one night entered the vicinity of one of the tourist camps. He had walked towards them and let off a shot with his rifle to scare them away. 'But', he added, 'I must admit, they didn't seem dangerous.' I said to him that surely his camps should be fenced considering how, due to the drought, lions and other animals were frequently being drawn to such camps for the artificial waterholes.

He replied that he would not consider fencing as this would spoil the 'ambience' of the camps and the 'experience' his guests enjoy. I told him that he was putting more emphasis on ambience than on the safety of tourists and wild animals which, because of the situation, could be brought into fatal contact with each other. This applied also to his staff 'compounds', which were also largely unfenced.

Also it was alleged that at the same camp, a manager had taken some tourists at night on foot towards my lions which had made a kill nearby. It was said that he had approached the pride, brandishing a portable spotlight. This behaviour could have resulted in the death of one or more of my lions if they had understandably charged the armed manager and the tourists, to deter them from the kill. Imagine the tourists' reaction if the lions had charged at them — chaos in the dark.

With this in mind we can return to the morning of 29 October 1992. Julie and I were heading down to the border in our old pick-up when the portable radio crackled. It was the 'manager', he told us that there was a major problem and that he wished to see us as soon as possible. We drove on, wondering what he wanted to see us about. When we parked at the offices, I saw a Tswana friend of mine. He looked concerned and said to me, 'Gareth, do you know about Isaac?' Isaac was a game scout working for the manager's organisation, an acquaintance with whom I used to chat about the Tuli lions, and my lions, whenever we met at the borderpost. I replied, 'No. What happened?' 'He and George Bale [another staff member] were walking last night to visit friends at Tuli Lodge,' he replied, 'and Isaac was attacked and killed by lions.' Blood must have visibly drained from our faces when we heard this. I then asked my friend for more details about the attack, such as which lion had attacked Isaac, how it had happened etc., but he said he did not know. The Tuli bushlands has a relatively small human community and when someone dies it is normally someone one knows, as was the case with Isaac. We then realised that this might be what the manager wanted to talk to us about — perhaps it was suspected that my lions were involved.

We then walked into the office. I thought of Furaha and where we suspected she and the cubs were. She could conceivably, though it was unlikely, have crossed to the extreme west of their range where the attack had reportedly taken place.

We soon met the manager and we

sat in his office as he told us what he knew about the attack. He told us in a calm tone that Isaac had left some camp staff the night before where they had sat around a fire, telling them that he was going to his room to sleep. According to those camp staff, that was the last time they saw him alive. They said at approximately 7.30 p.m. they heard a muffled sound 30 – 40 metres from where they sat. They told how they shone their torches in the direction of the sound and saw the reflecting eyes of lions. They said they thought the lions had made a kill and later they also went to their quarters to sleep.

In the morning, a ranger had set out on a game drive with two American clients. Some 800 metres south of the staff compound, he came across a group of lions. On driving closer, he saw that they were beside a body — a body of a man.

As we sat there, shocked, listening to these awful details, news was radioed in that trackers had established that spoor of three lions, one adult and two youngsters, was found near the camp and that a drag mark led to where Isaac's body was now lying.

Prior to this news, the manager was saying, 'We mustn't jump to conclusions. Perhaps Isaac was knocked on the head by someone.' The manager asked us where we thought Furaha was and added that he wished us to accompany him to where Isaac had been found, and to the area where it was thought that the lions were, so that if it was my lions which were 'responsible', I would be able to identify them.

We then drove north. I sat next to him in the front and Julie sat behind. He began saying it was a shame that it was Isaac who was dead as he was a good staff member and was to have been promoted to game ranger once he had got his driver's licence.

As I write this, I remember how we approached where Isaac's body lay by a back route, not along the conventional route to the tourist camp. The manager parked beside another vehicle where there stood an old man in a trench coat and a large man in a khaki uniform. The manager spoke to them both in Afrikaans before leading the way with the large man towards where Isaac's body lay. I followed, but waved Julie back. It was unnecessary for her to undergo seeing the body. The sight was horrific. The large man lifted a black plastic dustbin liner from the body — all that remained of the body was what could be covered by one plastic liner. I saw the body, then turned away. I saw his head, shoulders and below was bone. His flesh had been eaten. I also remember what was said by the large man as he uncovered the body. He said accusingly in Afrikaans as he indicated to the body, 'Ja, Gareth, daar's jou bok.' The literal translation being, 'Yes, Gareth, there's your buck (antelope).' In the haze of my shocked mind, those words burnt into me. Then and afterwards, I pondered upon the words, 'Daar's jou bok'.

I had not yet seen any lions, and certainly not confirmed that the lions in the vicinity were my pride. By this time, I was almost physically sick and I prayed that the lions we were about to search for would not be my pride. Julie, I knew, was feeling and thinking as I did.

205

We got into the vehicle again and, directed by the two men, headed to where the lions were thought to be. We moved on and I remember the manager commenting that he had not seen many dead people, but was again surprised to see how they quickly 'take on a rubbery look'.

A short time later, after continuing south, we crossed into an open area and near a shepherd's tree, I saw a single lioness. The manager stopped the vehicle approximately forty metres from her. I looked at the lioness, but strangely, perhaps because of shock, I do not know, I could not be sure whether it was Furaha or not. I asked Julie what she thought and she replied that she too was unsure. I called our (the lions') 'Aaowhey' — where are you? — call. What happened next almost broke my heart. The lioness called back to me, I had not instantly recognised her, but clearly she had recognised me. I began to tell myself it could still be another Tuli lioness responding to my lion call. Then I heard Julie saying to me, 'Go to her, Gareth, go to her'. Recently, I asked

Julie why she had said this. Firstly, she replied that if it had been another Tuli lioness, she would have fled as I got down from the vehicle and, secondly, if it was Furaha, I had to 'go to her'.

I stepped from the vehicle and vaguely heard the manager saying, 'You're mad. She's just killed a man.' I walked up to her in the silence that for the last time belonged to Furaha and me. I called her name. She called back, looking so confused. I crouched beside her and I felt helplessness — mine and hers — as though both of us sensed that nothing was going to prevent her from being destroyed, for a crime man deemed she had committed. The feeling between us was almost tangible and smothered us and all that was close to us. That is how I wished we could have remained, in our private world, in lion life. I said to her softly, 'Where are the cubs?' and looked around and saw no sign of them. Then the sight of the vehicle drew me out of lion life into the world of man. I stayed with her a little longer, reluctant to leave her.

When I left the vehicle, the manager

had turned to Julie and said, 'Are you sure it's OK? Are you sure?' Julie had told him, 'Yes'. He then watched Furaha and I together and, for a moment, Julie watched him. She later told me that on seeing Furaha and me together, he had looked 'strangely moved'. For those short moments, he was seeing for the first time and the last time the great depth of the relationship, the great love, between me and my lions.

I then rose and, after speaking softly to her, walked away. When I got back into the vehicle, tears welled up, but did not fall. Through the blur, I looked at Furaha for what I knew would be the last time ever in this life.

The manager drove back to where Isaac's mutilated body lay, then gave instructions to the two men before continuing on. I saw then, for the second time, the clear drag marks upon the ground leading from the staff compound down below almost a kilometre away. Tracks generally were hard to see because of the rocky ground and of course because of the rain that had fallen. I thought to myself, 'Why would they drag him so far from where he was killed?' I thought too, 'There were no signs of blood on Furaha's mouth, cheeks or whiskers', but those questions were soon lost in the daze of my mind. They were thoughts though that would be resurrected in the days ahead.

Julie and I were in shock and, because of this, strangely unquestioning that perhaps Furaha and the cubs were not responsible for Isaac's death. We were *told* what had happened, *told* what the trackers had said, TOLD! I will always blame myself that I did not snap out of my terror to view the picture more clearly. It was fixed in my mind that it was a hopeless situation, that it was inevitable that Furaha, Sala and Tana would be shot — that is the law if an animal kills a man. There was nothing I could do to prevent this. I remember thinking though that 'surely only the lion responsible should be shot'. I so wish I had pursued this instead of allowing the haze to cloud my thoughts with, 'but how would it be proven which lion had inflicted the mortal injury?' If I had thought this through further,

I personally would have inspected the site where it was alleged Isaac had been killed and there my tracking eyes could have uncovered other signs which might have had a bearing on the case in defence of the lions.

We rattled down the road to the border and the manager's offices. Along the way, a police vehicle approached. It drew up beside us and I saw my friend, Sergeant Tau ('tau' ironically means 'lion') climb out of the vehicle. He looked at me with great sadness when the manager said, 'It was Gareth's lions'. Tau had long been a supporter of mine, treasured his copies of my books and was fascinated by my relationship with lions. Tau understood my grief for he felt some of it too.

The lions had been tried and sentenced already. I felt as though Julie, myself, Furaha and the cubs were in a vacuum where we could scream but would never be heard. We were voiceless. For once, I was unable to speak on the lions' behalf. My God! Why didn't I question what was only circumstantial evidence, not proof?

At the office, I saw Mr Mazunga, a warden of the Department of Wildlife.

He too looked upset and said, 'Gareth, you know there is nothing you can do. You know what must happen now.' He then left with his game scouts, heading towards the tourist camp with their semi-automatic weapons to await the time of execution.

Pathetically, all it seemed I could do for my lions was maintain that they should be destroyed as humanely as possible. The Game Department staff in my experience were appalling shots. I told the manager about this and that his people must ensure that my lions died without prolonged pain, terror and anguish. In reply, he told me that his people would do the deed.

As we were preparing to leave, he then brought up Rafiki's name and said she must be shot or removed from the area. 'No!,' I retorted. 'She's done nothing. She was not with them last night, I have proof, she's on an eland kill just below my camp.' I have no explanation as to why he brought up the subject of Rafiki. The law indicates that only those animals responsible for a human death must be destroyed. His statement, I felt, was unjustified and irrelevant.

The battle for Rafiki's continued freedom had just begun.

★ ★ ★

Neither Julie nor I can remember much of the rest of the day. I vaguely remember phoning the Deputy Director of Wildlife, Mr Nchunga, about the matter. He was the man who had kindly sanctioned my proposal to bring the lions down from Kenya after George's murder. Now he was forced to sanction the death sentence of one of those lions and the two young ones born in their mother's new land. He, like us and others, were victims, all reacting to what we were TOLD had occurred. Everything happened too quickly, and if someone — me, the police, the Deputy Director, someone — had said, 'Slow down. Let's re-check the facts, do a post-mortem on the body to confirm cause of death, bring in independent trackers to investigate the signs and tracks, before shooting the lions.' Instead, it seemed that by instantly finding the lions guilty on circumstantial evidence alone, and destroying them, the case would be sealed. And then it would be in the past and life would carry on.

That evening, we found ourselves at Bruce Petty's house. Bruce was the warden of the Charter Reserve portion of the bushlands. Although Bruce and I had opposing views on, for example, management of the bushlands, he was always objective when it came to the lions and supported the rehabilitation project. He had always acknowledged that it had been a success. The lions lived predominantly in the Charter area and in four years, Bruce had said that day, he had no reason, based on observations, to claim that my lions were any more potentially dangerous to man than other Tuli lions.

When we arrived, Bruce had already heard much of the news on the area's radio network and was deeply disturbed by what he knew. I told him what we had experienced and he was very sympathetic and upset for Furaha and the cubs.

I had told the manager that we would be at Bruce's camp when he and the others set out to destroy my lions and

I told him too that I wished to be informed on the radio afterwards. We, with Bruce's wife and her friend, sat in their house awaiting the news. Eventually, the radio crackled and the manager called for me. With shaking hands, I lifted the microphone and replied. He said, 'It's over. They're dead. All head and neck shots.' I replaced the receiver, then my body shook with great heaving convulsions. Julie put her arms around me as I cried and cried. She did not allow herself to cry as, always giving, she felt that to allow herself to cry would not help me. She kept control for me. Bruce had looked terribly distressed, Julie told me later. I was informed two days later that after the fatal shots hit my lions, the Game Department rangers had fired a volley of shots into their bodies.

My memory becomes vague now. I do not remember what I said in Bruce's house, nor Julie's and my conversation as we left, driving through the drizzle, to our camp which, for the first time, I did not want to live in. The camp now was one of ghosts, ghosts of my lions' memory. Rafiki was now alone.

The following morning and for days afterwards, we would drive down to the border and cross to the cable car shed to make telephone calls. There was much to be done and responded to. Julie's support had, over the long months before, been unconditional — and now I needed that support so much.

We called those close to us to tell them what had happened. The first morning after the lions were killed, I phoned my friend and a trustee of the Tuli Lion Trust, Rozanne Savory. She was initially surprised to hear from me as she was on holiday in England. She broke down, sobbing, as I told her the news.

Julie and I felt we had an obligation to put together a media release. The lions' story was so well known by the public in Southern Africa. We had nothing to hide. At the same time, we worried that we would not be able to cope emotionally with the response and the inevitable flood of questions — similar to the response we had experienced after Batian's death.

I had thought that the manager would have immediately issued a press release, but he had not. I went to him and said

215

that perhaps he and I should consider doing a joint press release. He did not think this was a good idea. In addition, he began laying blame on all who had given permission for the lions to be brought to the bushlands, particularly the Landowners' Association. When I later informed him that I had issued our press release, he reacted with shock and soon issued his own which condemned my work and stated that the 'alleged' incident had occurred because my lions were 'tame' which, in reality, could not have been further from the truth.

The manager's press release was damning, and stated that the tragedy had been forced upon his organisation. He claimed that his organisation had consistently objected to the introduction of my lions into the bushlands.[1] Never, though, had they confronted me directly with this view. He claimed also that his organisation had been severely criticised in 'certain quarters' for expressing its concerns about the project. Who the

[1] *Citizen Newspaper*, 6 November 1992.

'certain quarters' were I did not know. It was certainly not us.

He went on to say that it was unnecessary to bring 'alien' lions into the bushlands where he stated the resident lions were already in equilibrium with their environment. This was factually wrong. In reality, when I brought my lions into the bushlands, the Tuli lion population was unstable due primarily to the lack of protection being afforded by the landowners which allowed poaching, illegal hunting and conflict with livestock owners to take its toll on the population. At the time of the alleged incident, the population was seriously depleted.

It was the manager's view that my dead lions had long been condemned to death by 'the very people who, in good faith, were attempting to return them to the wild'. These were patronising tones and again inaccurate. My lions had been *successfully* returned to the wild. Also, he was forgetting that only one lion which had been destroyed, Furaha, had been rehabilitated by me. Sala and Tana were at the time of their deaths over a year old and had been born in these wilds and raised by their mothers in the same wilds — not by me.

The manager was quoted in a separate news report, suggesting that it was known that Furaha was responsible for the incident. 'We believe the lioness (named Furaha by Mr Adamson) grabbed him . . . we found him a distance from the camp . . . The animal was sitting on top of him, eating him.'[1] I had seen no blood on her mouth, cheeks or whiskers, despite the fact that the incident had taken place only two hours earlier, there was no evidence that she had been eating him. But it was stated, 'Isaac Mangogola was killed on the night of October 29th, close to his living quarters, by *three tame Patterson lions.*'

Just before sending out my own press release, I had informed a member of the Landowners' Association of my intention. I was told that under no circumstances was I to send out the release. I replied that I had nothing to hide and had an obligation to inform the public. To this,

[1] *Cape Times*, 5 November 1992.

I was told I was making 'scarcely veiled accusations' at the manager's organisation and this would not be tolerated. I was then told I must get out of the bushlands, close down my project and that Rafiki must be removed too.

It was a few days after the deaths of Isaac, Furaha and the cubs that I sent out my carefully prepared release. Enough time had passed for me to begin to think rationally about why in fact the incident had actually occurred. Why would my lions have attacked Isaac? What had prompted them to do so? I tried to piece together the circumstances from the lions' view, according to what we had been told. This was a first step towards what was to become a long, painful, often scary, journey towards the truth.

My early conclusions were that the (alleged) attack had occurred because of Isaac's squatting position. We had been told that after leaving the others by the fire, he had in fact walked some thirty-five metres into the bush to defecate. From many examples, and from what I had seen at first-hand, I knew that the squatting position of humans elicits threatening (or rather, defensive) behaviour in many predators. I had, for example, witnessed that Sala and Tana would become immediately agitated and would growl if I crouched at a medium distance, but would relax when I stood upright. When I was attacked by a leopard (and my life had been saved by Furaha who had leapt over me in defence and seized it), I was in a crouched position. (She had saved my life and yet I had been unable to save her's.)

There are other examples: a female friend of mine rather foolishly left a vehicle to urinate next to it in the vicinity of a Tuli lion pride. At first, there was no response from the lions . . . until she squatted. Then a young lion immediately began stalking her. Marks Owens, in *Cry of the Kalahari*, recounts an experience with a wild dog pack: 'when I squatted, the mood of the pack suddenly changed, . . . stalked towards me. I stood up. The effect was immediate. The entire pack relaxed.'

Lastly, I was told how film-maker, Richard Goss, witnessed a similar situation while with hyaenas which were feeding on a gemsbok in the Kalahari. When he filmed standing up, the hyaenas did not respond, but as he attempted low angle shots, shifting to a crouching position, the hyaenas immediately reacted in a threatening way.

My early conclusion, therefore, was that Isaac could have been attacked because of the lions' interpretation of his posture — reacting to his body language as the predators mentioned above also reacted.

In my statement, I made it clear that the situation — Isaac's death and my lions' death — could have been avoided if the camp had been fenced, thus the lions would not have been within the camp area. I also mentioned that in April the year before, I had sent a memorandum to the Landowners' Association calling for the fencing of tourist camps and staff quarters. This I did because potentially dangerous animals were, according to my observations, being drawn to camps due to the drought situation and the game's reliance on water at the artificial waterholes.

I also stated that, recognising these

increasing dangers, I had personally, from my own resources, provided fencing for camps and staff quarters in the Charter portion of the bushlands. I wished it to be made clear that, contrary to the manager's opinion, the incident had not occurred because Furaha was a lion raised by man and rehabilitated back to the wilds. I knew her best, and she was, in response to humans, as wild as any other Tuli lion. She had lived free and independent of me for over two and a half years and in that time, never did her behaviour indicate that she was more of a threat to humans than other lions.

I ask now, if she was a man-eater why was the camp manager who, with his guests, approached my lions on foot, not attacked? Why had there never been any previous attacks by my lions who not unfrequently saw people walking or cycling through the bushlands? Reports given to me by people who had come across my lions on foot always indicated the opposite — that they were non-aggressive and would move away shyly into the bush. Remember too the incident recounted earlier when a crowd of adults and children got out of a vehicle and approached the eland kill when my lions were nearby.

I stated that I felt Furaha and the cubs had reacted instinctively to a threat made inadvertently to them. Isaac was dead. So too were the lions. It was a grave tragedy which, I thought, could in part have been avoided.

Later I followed up these conclusions as to why the alleged attack had taken place by undertaking a small survey on the man/animal conflicts that had occurred at two camps in the bushlands. I then sent my findings to the Director of Wildlife & National Parks, Nigel Hunter, who was now having pressure put on him by the Landowners' Association to have Rafiki removed from the area or shot.

In my survey, I found that no fences existed at the camps, one of which had a waterhole situated nearby. Staff members were forced to squat in the bush to defecate as there were no toilets or washing facilities. They were in particular danger as lions regularly visited one of the camps. I also discovered that a big male lion had recently bounded onto an upturned wheelbarrow which had been left beside a cooking fire, not three metres from the staff's dwelling. Tracks of a lion pride were found all around the tiny three by three metre dwelling in which the staff member lived with his wife and small child. Each night, they were forced to use a tin to urinate in for fear of venturing outside.

I also discovered that just days after the deaths of Isaac and my lions, an illegal immigrant crossing the bushlands, to South Africa from Zimbabwe, had been surrounded by the Shashe pride. It was full moon and, terrified, he had thrashed out with a stick to keep the lions away as he headed to the 'safety' of the above-mentioned camp. There, the camp staff were too afraid to open the door of the little dwelling because of the man's screams. The illegal immigrant, in a desperate attempt to get away from the lions, climbed into a tree and remained there the entire night. He was found in the morning and tracks verified his story.

In my report, I cited other examples of how people, due to lack of camp fencing *and* toilet facilities, were constantly in danger of coming into conflict with potentially dangerous wild animals — all information I felt was relevant, especially after what had allegedly occurred the night of Isaac's death. I felt more than ever that my calling for camp fencing in the bushlands the year before had been a warning. Now that an incident had occurred, fencing was imperative. I felt too that such information in turn highlighted that there was no justification for having Rafiki shot or removed from the bushlands.

Increasingly, I realised that she was becoming the scapegoat, and that I was being forced to leave the bushlands.

10

Tears of Mourning

EACH day for almost two weeks, our routine was to drive down to the border, cross it and then spend hours making and receiving telephone calls dealing with the alleged incident. It was November, and temperatures were soaring, it was in the mid-forties inside the corrugated iron cable car shed where our telephone was. In the afternoon, we would wearily cross back into Botswana and drive for an hour and a quarter to our camp.

On each return, I would wait expectantly for Rafiki who might appear in the evenings or late in the night. Whenever she did appear, before greeting her, I would wonder whether she had sensed the death of her sister and the cubs. Inevitably, she did learn of their passing, expressing severe grief, of which I will write further on. She was at the time ranging north of her territory, accompanied by Nelion, the fine young male who so resembled Batian. Sometimes, they mated close to camp and at night on these occasions, we would hear their courtship snarls, rumbling purrs and growls.

At the time of the deaths and in the months ahead, I do not think we would have coped without the support of one person in particular, Alpheus Marupane. Alpheus was a close friend, a tall, dignified and kind Tswana man who ran a small supply store in the bushlands, as well as managing a camp along the Limpopo river.

One day, as the time of Isaac's funeral drew close, Alpheus told us that he wished to accompany us and be with us on that day. We appreciated his offer, as although we knew it was imperative and right that we should attend the funeral, we were unsure how Isaac's family and close friends might react to us emotionally — would we be blamed? The night before the funeral, Julie and I stayed with Alpheus so that we might leave early to make our way together to the village where Isaac was to be buried.

The following morning, after an hour's drive, we reached the village and parked amongst the many cars near Isaac's home. We began looking for Peter Senamolela among the crowds of people, our game warden friend who days previously had sent us a message saying that we should attend the funeral. Peter spotted us first and soon approached us. After greeting us, Peter said quietly to me, 'It is good you have come. It shows you have nothing to hide, and that you are not avoiding Isaac's family.'

Many of the faces around us were those of our friends and acquaintances from the bushlands and softly they would greet us or nod in our direction. Throughout the funeral proceedings, Alpheus always remained close by, guiding us to where we were to go. He was a quiet but supportive presence.

As we approached the entrance to Isaac's cluster of traditional huts, we suddenly saw his coffin being loaded into a pick-up. Immediately, my mind flashed back to when I had seen his remains and I thought how pathetically light the contents of the coffin must be. The image of his remains is imprinted on my mind forever.

Family, friends and acquaintances of Isaac then climbed into vehicles which formed a procession behind that carrying the coffin. We — Alpheus, Peter, Julie and I — got into the back of a pick-up and were driven slowly to the small cemetery on the outskirts of the village. With the crowds, we then gathered around the freshly dug grave. Over a thousand people had come to pay their last respects to Isaac. His coffin was placed near the grave and the crowd was told to be seated on the ground. Our regional MP, James Maruatona, then rose to speak. He said that with the development of a country and its industries, inevitably and regrettably accidents involving human life would occur and Isaac's death was an example of this. He gave his condolences to Isaac's family and said that after the grieving, life would have to carry on. After his speech, the village chief, who was also Isaac's uncle, rose and spoke.

He said, amongst many things, that he did not entirely agree with what James Maruatona had said, stating that Isaac's death could have been prevented and he felt that perhaps there was accountability for what had occurred. After his speech, Peter stood up. He was representing the country's Wildlife Department and said his staff, upon hearing of the incident, had acted promptly. He told how the lions had been brought to Botswana with his department's approval, and that the rehabilitation project had their support, but it was immensely regrettable that such an incident had occurred. Peter then motioned to me in the crowd to stand to be recognised as the person who had brought the lions to Botswana. He did so to show that it was not thought by him that I was in any way responsible for what had happened.

I stood up from the dusty ground and saw hundreds of faces turn in my direction. Some looked at me with familiarity, others looked, then faced the ground. Only in a few were there flickers of anger and resentment, but the crowd's overall reaction was a testament to the integrity of those people that day. The majority bore me no malice — but also some, I feel, perhaps had a greater insight than I as to what had actually happened that night.

I was then motioned to sit down again. What Peter spoke about next, I shall never forget. Peter told of my lions being shot and I closed my eyes as he told the crowd that they were then skinned and their bodies burnt.

All this time, there was a relative calm in the crowd. The outflow of emotions was now about to take place and did so as Isaac's coffin was lowered into the grave. As the first handful of soil was thrown on to the coffin, hysterical screaming from women members of Isaac's family shook the air. Dust rose as mourners in turn shovelled soil into the grave. The air and my mind seemed filled with the same haze. The screams, the tears, the haze were all parts of the song of sadness pervading everywhere. The scene had a sense of unreality. It was as though I was trapped within a dream from which I could not awake. Julie stood next to me, completely still and quiet. Alpheus stood a little ahead, taller than most. With his hands sunk deep into the pockets of his jacket, his face a mask, he looked on.

To my left stood a female friend of myself and Isaac. She stood singly, crying alone and she so mirrored my own emotions that I was rooted, unable to go to her and comfort her.

I was focused upon Death — Isaac's death, George's death, that of Batian, Furaha and the cubs. I felt my own death and saw these same people, my many Tswana friends, gathered around my own grave — next to Batian's in the bushlands. I saw my own burial that day. I saw myself watching my own funeral, my spirit moving unseen amongst my mourning friends. What I saw there was almost like a premonition — or, perhaps, a response to shock and the occasion . . . ?

★ ★ ★

After the burial, with the rest of the crowd, we returned to Isaac's family's home. There I thought of his children. No words can describe how I actually felt. We were led to seats next to James Maruatona, the MP. It was then that we were to be snapped out of our private thoughts and brought back to reality.

To digress a little. Prior to the funeral, it was rumoured that a letter written by Isaac had been found in his quarters after his death. In that letter, we were told, he described that he felt his life was in danger.

James turned to me and told me he had seen this letter and was disturbed by its contents. I realised that this was no mere rumour. He told us that Isaac felt his life was in danger because of his knowledge of the unsolved case of a rifle which had been stolen from that camp. He had written the letter to his mother and we heard that just prior to his death, he wished to return to his home.

The impression was forming in our minds that he knew who was responsible for the theft of the rifle, and this knowledge endangered his life. The case was unsolved and it was reasonable to surmise that those who stole the rifle were still employed at that camp at the time of Isaac's death. No arrests had been made.

These were early thoughts — very early thoughts on which there was too little to make assumptions. After the funeral, I had to write a statement for Sergeant Tau of the police. I put away my early thoughts that foul play may have been the cause of Isaac's death and in my statement, I described why, given what I had been told, the lions may have attacked Isaac. I was accused because the incident had occurred as a result of Furaha having been a lion reared by man and returned to the wild. She was so-called 'tame' and it was alleged that she had no fear of man. I stated clearly in my statement that these accusations were not true and wrote about Isaac's posture, citing the examples of predators' reactions to humans squatting. This statement contributed to the closing of the case. Ironically, I had aided the prevention of further lines of investigation surrounding the case being explored. Weeks later, in part because of information I had gathered and presented to the authorities, the case was re-opened under 'alleged murder'.

It was ironical too that Furaha was

referred to as having been 'tame' — therefore of danger to man. The Collins dictionary definition of 'tame' is 'not wild, domesticated, subdued'. The question was raised later by the Deputy Director of Wildlife & National Parks — if she was 'tame', why would she be more of a danger to man?

At that time too, an important point relevant to the case was being missed by the authorities and me, and the point was the following. In his press release, the manager had stated that 'Isaac was an ardent naturalist and possessed a great love and knowledge of the bush and the fauna and flora occurring within it. He was a top member of our team . . . '. This I do not doubt. Isaac knew the lions were close to camp. His brother told me later that he and Isaac saw them in the vicinity towards sunset. In addition, it was known that they had made two kills over the previous two days (they were hardly starving). Taking this into account, why would a knowledgeable naturist wander alone without a torch and unarmed into the bush to defecate when it was known that there were lions nearby? The camp had toilet facilities. If he did do this, do his actions not contradict the manager's assessment of 'a top member of our team'? I do not think the manager's assessment is in question, because I do not believe that Isaac was in fact killed by the lions.

* * *

On 3 January 1980, Joy Adamson was found dead on a road near her camp in the Shaba Game Reserve. There were deep wounds in her chest, head and arms, and at first it was assumed she had been killed by a lion. Before she was cremated, a post-mortem was undertaken. It was revealed that in fact she had not been killed by a lion, but murdered — with a short stabbing knife.

On the morning of 6 September 1988, a young English woman, Julie Ward, disappeared in the Masai Mara Game Reserve. In the days that followed the eventual discovery of Julie's remains, blame for her death was laid on lions, leopards or a pack of hyaena. Her father's private investigation unearthed much, including that her remains had been burnt with the use of fuel. In turn, the Kenyan authorities were forced to retract the claim that wild animals were responsible for her death. The identity of her human killers was never established, but there seems little doubt that Julie was murdered.

Were Furaha, Sala and Tana killed for a crime they did not commit? As this tale unfolds, I feel you will understand why to this question today I answer 'Yes'. In Africa, as elsewhere, a human death often conceals truth. Animals are blamed and sentenced to death so easily, so casually, for they cannot speak for themselves, they have no defence presented on their behalf — and a human goes to the grave with the truth, sometimes for knowing too much. But the truth can rise from the grave. Man is not infallible. Time, I believe, is the ultimate provider of truth.

★ ★ ★

After the funeral, Julie and I were led to a house and presented to members of Isaac's family. We tried to express our

237

heartfelt sympathies and in turn were told that I was not blamed and that if the lions were responsible, to blame myself would be to blame a father for the actions of his offspring, and that this was wrong. Emotionally, I then read out to them a portion of a poem by Francis Nnaggenda:

The dead are not under the earth
They are in the tree that rustles
They are in the woods that groan
They are in the water that runs . . .
Those who are dead are never gone
They are in the child wailing and in
  the fire that flames . . .
When my ancestors talk about
  the Creator, they say:
He is with us . . . We sleep with him.
We hunt with him. We dance with him.

Then I cried, Julie cried and they cried. Peter was present and as I tried to stem my tears and wipe my eyes, he said to me from across the room, 'No, let it come out, Gareth, it is good.' I was feeling their loss and they were feeling mine. Later, we left the room with mutual, and almost tangible, understanding between us. The image of the women and children became indelible. We three — Julie, Alpheus and I — left the village heading towards the bushlands with our own silent thoughts.

★ ★ ★

Rafiki, driven by intuition, walked late one night towards the place of the deaths. Nelion walked behind her, perhaps not knowing or understanding why she was drawn to this place of man. He could see the lights of the camp flickering in the near distance. Rafiki reached the place where her sister, Furaha, had died. She stood where Tana's blood had spilt and where her own lion child, Sala, had lain as life had slipped away. Two days later, it was reported to me that the tracks of a lioness and a young male had been found where the deaths had occurred.

At this time, Julie had left the bushlands to be with her mother who was unwell in Johannesburg. Alone one evening, I heard a lion near the west-facing fence and I knew it was Rafiki. I went to her, still thinking that she was visiting me not knowing of the deaths. I forced positive thoughts into my head, as I always tried to do now when she visited. I did not want her to sense the troubled time.

I knew almost immediately that she now knew as she pressed her head against me, moaning loud tortured groans. As I tried to comfort her, I witnessed raw anguish and angry pain. Her sounds and actions were identical, but of greater intensity than those I had seen when she reacted to my impending departure from the old Tawana. Her grieving at the realisation of her family's deaths will haunt me and her forever. This was pain and it was to continue for a prolonged period.

Each evening, she would appear at my camp and, poor Fiks, she would in varying degrees react as she had that first evening, and each evening, I would try to comfort her as best I could. For her hurt, I pushed my own aside and responded to hers. I would try to push aside my mourning in long stretches during my fight to prevent

Rafiki from being shot, or removed from the bushlands which was the landowners' other request. My mourning period was also smothered as I attempted too to resolve what had actually occurred on that night of the 29th.

At dawn at the time of Rafiki's mourning, I would awake at sunrise, step from my tent and always find her asleep close by, normally pressed against the fence facing my tent. Each morning, I wished her not to hear me and awake, for once awoken, the anguished groans would begin as her loss re-surfaced. There, asleep, she was seemingly free of the hurt and at peace — vulnerable-looking, but at peace. Each morning, her raw sorrow would awake and the pain would be lived again until she slept once more.

I do not know where Nelion was at this time. Perhaps Rafiki wanted to be alone with me? I will never know. Time gradually passed and there were nights when she did not come to me and days dawned when I did not find her asleep close to me, and I knew she was beginning to spend more time with Nelion and I thanked God for his presence. In the weeks ahead, they mated and at last, life was again conceived within her.

Before she conceived, I, in the world of man, was fighting for her survival and future in the bushlands. Then, as life developed within her, I was fighting for the unborn cubs too, for the survival and future of those 'yet unborn'. I had had this realisation before. Months previously, after Batian's death and as I sat beside the stone cairn marking his grave, I saw around the cairn the little pugmarks of Rafiki's previous litter of cubs (which included Sala). I later wrote of this realisation: 'There around me was the answer to my questions . . . The future, and the future being living lions, little cubs and those of their kind yet unborn . . . and I drew my courage from a remarkable lion called Batian.' Now, for Rafiki and the unborn, I knew I had to try to draw courage from him again.

11

Towards Trails of Truth

BY the end of November, I was becoming more and more convinced that my lions were not responsible for Isaac's death. At the same time, calls were increasingly being made by the manager and the Landowners' Association to have Rafiki removed from the area or shot. I decided to write to the local police with my suspicions and did so, first and foremost because if Isaac had been murdered, the people responsible could easily kill again. I knew from conversations with local community members in the bushlands that I was not alone in my suspicions but others, who thought as I did, were too afraid to express their thoughts to the police. I must emphasise that the Tuli bushlands has a relatively small human population. It's a small community with everyone knowing everyone else either directly or indirectly. The only other person who to my knowledge came forward to speak to the police was my friend, Bane Sesa, who was then Chief Immigration Officer for the area. He had been away at the time of the deaths, but on his return, he immediately requested a meeting with me. In the months ahead, Sesa worked closely with me in unravelling what we could, and we uncovered much important information.

The fact that Isaac and my lions were dead was awful, but the thought that Isaac might have been murdered and that Furaha, Sala and Tana had been killed for a crime they did not commit was horrendous — and frightening. I did, however, feel that if this was proven, then surely there was no justification for having Rafiki removed from the bushlands. Today I realise such thinking was naïve. The situation was being manipulated.

Before compiling my letter to the police, I looked into as many documented cases of lion/predator attacks on humans as possible. What became startlingly evident was the lack of similarity between what was said to have occurred on the night of the 29th and what was documented in the cases I unearthed. I discovered that almost all the cases had two main common denominators: first, severe injuries, those that would have been the cause of death, are normally inflicted to the neck and head of the victim. Second, on being attacked, the victim screams loudly, and is often heard by people in the vicinity. Both upper body injuries and screams were absent in Isaac's case.

In my report, I stressed both these aspects. The doctor's post-mortem report, which I saw later and read for myself, confirmed one of the points — there was no mention of upper body injuries. One must remember that the most common method used by lions to kill prey is strangulation/suffocation, or a bite to the back of the neck which results in crushed upper vertebrae and death. Alternatively, when man is the victim, the severing of the carotid artery is often the cause. In addition, what was not stated in the post-mortem report was the actual cause of death and unfortunately what was also missing was the estimated time of death.

This, I feel, would have revealed much.

Regarding the screams, it was said that Isaac was only thirty-five metres from the staff camp when the alleged attack occurred, but no one reported hearing any screams or cries. One of George Adamson's lions, Boy, killed a man and George's own words recount what occurred — and this should be borne in mind in relation to Isaac's death: 'We heard terrified cries from behind . . . as soon as I got out of the back gate, I saw Boy with Stanley in his mouth about 250 yards away.' George shot Boy and it is stated that once Boy had bitten Stanley, he had no chance of survival. A tooth had severed his jugular and he died in less than ten minutes.

The man's cries were heard from a distance of 250 yards, and the man died from a severed jugular and extreme blood loss (which was not mentioned in Isaac's case). In the many other cases I investigated, words pertaining to screams or cries and upper body injuries leapt up at me because of their absence in Isaac's case. The following are examples and come from a myriad of separate cases:

Women heard the man call. 'Lion has got me.'

Villagers were brought to the spot by the victim's cries for help.

For a quarter of an hour, he called for help while the animal was eating him alive.

His yells vibrated horribly through the night.

At Letaba, a black man was bitten in the head and later died.

. . . was attacked and savaged by a lion sustaining severe lacerations in the face . . .

When George's assistant was attacked by a lion, George recounted the 'deep gashes in his neck, head and arms' and 'formidable puncture scars around the neck'.

In addition, the fact that Isaac's body was found over 800 metres from where he was allegedly attacked seemed unusual if the lions were indeed responsible. Why would lions drag a body such a distance over rocky terrain at night before eating him? I cannot understand this. Never in the four years I lived intimately with my lions, often being with them when kills were made, had I observed them dragging prey anything like such extreme distances.

Also, Isaac was of average build, weighing roughly the same as an impala. An impala would be consumed by an adult lioness and two large cubs in a short time. In this case, it was alleged they were still eating him thirteen hours after they had killed him. I came to the conclusion that in fact the lions had actually come across his body many hours after he had died — probably attracted by the activity of smaller scavengers, such as jackal, who had eaten most of his body.

This is reinforced by my observations on many occasions when I came across impala which had died in a large-scale snaring area. As with Isaac, only the neck and head would often still be intact. Most of the flesh would be absent with only larger body bones remaining. In the night, the jackals would have stripped the carcass.

I put all this forward to the local police. Some time later, I was requested by the local police to submit the information to the head of the CID at the town of Selibe Phikwe. This I did, and it resulted in the weeks ahead in the case being re-opened under 'alleged murder'. I remember telling a senior police official at the case's re-opening that perhaps I could be wrong in my assumptions and I was told, 'But, Gareth, you could be very right . . . ' This, I must stress, was to happen only in the weeks ahead.

Two days after sending my initial report to the local police, a very strange occurrence took place — an occurrence that was a form of confirmation of what I had suspected had happened on the night of the 29th. A close friend of mine, who had been very upset by the whole situation, had, unbeknown to me, consulted a psychic medium who was regarded as being extremely accurate. Simply and without any elaboration or detail, my friend said to the medium, 'A lioness has been shot for killing a man. What can you tell me?'

During the consultation, the medium said, 'He is with us, and he says he was murdered. That the lions had nothing to do with it.' The medium became unsettled as she said that a man and his girlfriend were also in danger. 'Their lives are in danger. They must both leave the area.' She went on to say that there were two or three men involved in Isaac's death and she gave their initials.

Over the phone, my friend told me about this. At first, I was a little sceptical and asked how much detail she had given the medium. She replied firmly, 'only that a lioness had been shot for killing a man'. I then thought it remarkable and frightening. My friend then became agitated. 'You two must leave the Tuli, Gareth.' Recently, I asked her what my response had been and she said, 'You wouldn't hear of it.'

At the end of our conversation, I asked my friend to make an appointment for me to see the medium. I had to hear for myself and to hear more. Pondering on what I had been told, I then drove back to camp. I was becoming increasingly alarmed and at first was unsure what to tell Julie, but of course I had to tell her and did so later at camp.

Julie does not 'fear' in the conventional sense. She does not hold fears, as such, for herself. However, she would continually hold fears for me in the bush — that I could become involved in life-threatening encounters with elephants, other lions, leopard or snakes — or poachers. But she never seemed to fear for her own life. In fact, I have seen her show no fear even during a dangerous situation. It is a trait in her personality, always worrying about others rather than herself. It runs parallel with her continually giving of herself to others — often at a cost to herself.

When I told her about my earlier conversation with my friend, she immediately became concerned for me, particularly as she knew I would at that time never leave the bushlands. This would have been tantamount to deserting Rafiki. I suggested, for her own safety's sake, that she consider leaving for a while. True to form, she did not want to discuss this option and concentrated on the possible threats to me.

Prior to hearing what the medium had said, we had already begun to express our thoughts to others as to what could actually have occurred on the night of the 29th. Putting them on paper for the police had been a way of formalising our doubts, and at a meeting to take place in Gaborone concerning Rafiki's future, we indicated that we were not convinced that the lions had in fact been responsible for Isaac's death.

The meeting had been called by the Director of Wildlife & National Parks, Nigel Hunter, and was attended by ourselves, the manager, the Deputy Director and other officials. During the meeting, I said that it was unfair that Rafiki's future should be tied to the 'incident' even if Furaha had been responsible. I stated that she was completely innocent and I could prove that she was near my camp on the night of the 29th. That meeting was the first time that it became apparent what indeed was going on in the big picture. The Furaha and Isaac situation was being used as a means of not so much removing Rafiki from the bushlands, but rather me. This realisation was to become crystal clear in the time to come.

During the meeting, Julie spoke up saying, 'Everyone's blaming Furaha', and added that it had not been conclusively proven that Furaha was guilty. The response was uneasy laughter, the kind of laughter that could be a reaction to the possibility that just perhaps things are not as they seem. It seemed that the seeds of doubt had already been sown in the minds of those attending the meeting.

I said that if indeed the lions were responsible, then perhaps the issue of camp fencing should be raised. I said that I had warned the landowners of potential human/animal conflict due to lack of fencing a year previously. I asked why the manager had electrified strands around his own house, but staff on at least two of his camps had absolutely no fencing whatsoever. At this point, the meeting became heated. The manager said that if one has a dog that is dangerous, one has the responsibility of preventing contact with people, 'and to keep it locked up'. I replied that Furaha and the cubs were lions, wild-living lions, and that they were not domesticated. I reminded him of the words he had said weeks earlier, that 'they didn't seem dangerous'.

The Director said that his department had also incurred loss of human life as a result of lion and other wild animal attacks, and he said that only the animal responsible for human death is shot, not the entire pride. This indicated that by rights, nothing should be done to Rafiki. He concluded the meeting by saying that the matter should receive further attention and that a meeting with all the members of the Landowners' Association would be called to determine whether Rafiki's future was an 'area' decision.

Rafiki's future now seemed tied to the laws and rights of land ownership. Technically, like all wild animals in Botswana, she belonged to the state, but the bushlands belonged to private landowners and it seemed that if they perceived a particular animal as being dangerous or undesirable, they had the right to call on the Department to deal with the matter. This was why the Director wanted an 'area' consensus before a decision was made. Privately, the Director was clearly sympathetic to our — and Rafiki's — situation. Even then, he too could see the true motivation of some of the landowners. In fact, he even said to me later, 'Don't fight the land issue through Rafiki.' He was referring to my continual emphasis on the lack of wildlife protection by the landowners.

During, before and after the meeting, he also made the point to all that if Rafiki had been in one of his National Parks, his Department would not have reason to take action against her. But sadly, Rafiki, Furaha and the cubs were not, for many reasons, in a protected National Park, but in a game area which was privately owned and this seemed to make the situation quite different. This underscored to me much of what was wrong with the Tuli bushlands and its wildlife.

The (state's) wildlife was being inadequately protected with an untold number of animals dying annually. This was reinforced by Rafiki's situation. She was on private land, and therefore was not as guarded as those lions in National Parks are where the law provides protection. The lack of wildlife protection in the bushlands meant that there was a lack of legislation enforcing private landowners to be responsible guardians of the state's wildlife which is resident on their land. This must change since it is affecting one of the country's national resources.

Ownership could be defined as 'possessing', but how many of us would like to be 'possessed'? 'Land ownership', and particularly 'ownership' of wilderness in all reality is an arrogant man-created myth. How can an individual 'own' the wilds? It was there before him and will be there after him. I do not believe you can be an 'owner' of the wilds, but you can be its custodian, its guardian. If anything, before we coined the notion of 'ownership', the wilds held proprietorship over us! When man lived in the wilds as a component of the wilds — of no greater or lesser importance than lions, zebras or termites — the wilds provided for us. The difference between today and yesterday is that reverence for the wilds and all life, once held by us, has been lost. If we wish to, we can glean and understand from those minorities who still hold this reverence . . . the native American Indians, the last Bushmen, the last true Australian Aborigines. What is sacred cannot be owned, and to me the wilds are sacred.

Throughout this book, I term the lions 'my' lions. The 'my' is a term of affection and love and not one indicating ownership. Never did I feel that the lions belonged to me. The thought never crossed my mind and did not, I suppose, because our relationship was in part based upon respect. Those of wild hearts cannot be owned if we heed natural law. Perhaps I am overstating my point, but the definition of human ownership applied to the wilds baffles me. I cannot grasp the notion. I cannot see how a single grain of sand from a riverbed or a fallen leaf upon the ground, or a hill or a fish eagle high in the sky can be 'owned' — be a possession of man. What I feel, however, did not unfortunately alter the situation regarding Rafiki, and the meeting where her future was to be decided quickly approached.

The meeting of some of the landowners and the Director took place early in December in Johannesburg. My friend and a Trustee of the Tuli Lion Trust,

Rozanne Savory, also attended. She brought with her a document she had prepared which detailed facts and theories concerning Isaac's death, and a conclusion which cast doubt that Furaha and the cubs had been responsible for Isaac's death. I brought along a statement from a Tswana friend, Jippy, who was the caretaker of an unfenced camp through which my and other lions would pass. Jippy saw my lions in the bush on more occasions than any landowner and I felt his comments were important when assessing the lions' behaviour.

The meeting was not attended by all those individuals who own land in the bushlands, which meant that any decision made would not be democratically representative of the area. Again, what I felt did not matter. In fact, the decision concerning Rafiki had already been made by those who wished to see her and me leave the bushlands.

As we gathered for the meeting, Rozanne approached the Director and as they began talking, she handed him a copy of the document she had prepared. A senior member of the Landowners'

Association saw this and stepped forward quickly. He asked Rozanne to take her seat as the meeting was about to start — effectively cutting off any further conversation between the Director and herself.

From the beginning, the meeting was heading in only one direction. Rafiki would have to go. I then said that I wanted to read Jippy's statement, explaining why I thought it was important and relevant. As I read the statement, I was interrupted several times by the same senior member. I continued nevertheless and tried not to be distracted by his interruptions where he felt that I'd spoken enough. Jippy's statement was critical as he had pointed out that my lions and other lions came to the vicinity of the camp because of the artificial waterholes, but never had he experienced any trouble whatsoever. He also stated that lions were drawn to his previously unfenced staff camp where he lived with his wife and two children 'to take my meat rations'. He wrote 'I told my boss about this problem and they gave me a temporary fence. But now my compound is safe because Gareth gave me a real fence.' The statement continued, 'Gareth's lions are just the same as others here in the bush' and he repeated that never had he had reason to complain because of my lions' actions. Sadly, in reality, what Jippy stated or thought didn't matter one iota at this meeting. There wasn't any visible response from the landowners to a grass-roots, first-hand opinion about the lions. Perhaps a difference would have been made, though only perhaps, if the warden of the Charter Reserve, Bruce Petty, had attended the meeting or had sent his own statement. Bruce had in fact been deterred by some of his landowner employers from doing either.

Bruce could have told all at the meeting that in his experience, as warden of the area most frequented by my pride, he had no reason to believe that my lions were any more dangerous to man than other lions. He could also have stated that my lions had never shown aggressive or threatening behaviour to him or his staff. He could have told everyone present that he felt the rehabilitation project had been worthwhile and a success. Finally, he could have told them that both he and I realised that in the exceptional drought conditions, lions were more frequently being drawn to camps. We had acted responsibly by fencing almost all the staff camps in the Charter Reserve. Bruce was not present though, and thus none of the above was mentioned.

The Managing Director of the tourist operation where Isaac had worked then spoke, saying that he would put ten thousand rand aside for the erection of an enclosure. Rafiki would be held in it until such time as she could be taken away from the area. He said that once it had been used to hold Rafiki, it could be used for the area's benefit in future for holding captured game destined for sale.

Some of the landowners nodded their approval and the same senior member said that this was a very generous gesture and much appreciated. I was absolutely horrified and appalled. Rafiki was pregnant with cubs. She had known only freedom and would be horribly stressed if imprisoned. I said this and told the man to use the R10,000 to fence his staff compounds to protect those who worked for him. Towards the end of the meeting, it was inevitably decided that Rafiki must be moved and that in the interim period of two months, I was to find an alternative reserve for her. In the meantime, I had to monitor her closely and supply her with impala carcass baits in order to keep her as close to my camp as possible. The Director had actually proposed that she merely be radio-collared, together with another Tuli lion, so that a comparative survey could be conducted to see whether she moved through camps more often than the other collared lion. If this was the case, then a decision would have to be made. The landowners would not agree to this, stating simply that they wanted her 'out'.

One of the Charter owners became very aggressive towards me, showing unrestrained behaviour which was certainly not missed by the Director. Hearing this man's words, I burned with anger and said that it was clear that the landowners' real agenda here was, in truth, to get me out of the bushlands. I told them that once I had found a new home for Rafiki, I would return and remain in the bushlands. There was silence. This was not what they had expected. They had assumed I would go with Rafiki and not return. Then the senior member said hesitantly, 'Er, what private arrangements have you made to stay?' His words then trailed off. I did not answer. The atmosphere, his words, the others' heated retorts were all a damning admission of what their real motive was. They wanted to be rid of me. They had forgotten that my fight was not only for my lions or the Tuli lions alone, but for all the bushlands and its presently vulnerable wild inhabitants.

After the meeting, I went up to the Director. He was sad for us and expressed his disappointment that there was little that he could do once the landowners had decided that Rafiki must be removed from their land. He had again seen for himself the real issue. 'If only the Tuli was a National Park', I thought as I left. Then Rafiki would simply be left alone and would not be caught up as a victim of the politics of men.

* * *

That same day, in the afternoon, I had my consultation with the medium. As I sat there, to my astonishment, she first repeated almost identically what she had told my friend. She told me that Isaac had been murdered, that he warned that our lives were in danger. She said to me, 'You're not alone up there . . . your girlfriend . . . I think at least you must get her out of there.' She said that if I stayed on, I must be constantly on guard and armed. Things became more frightening when she said, 'You could be attacked by two men. They will come for you from behind.' When I asked about Rafiki, she said that she must be moved or 'she too will be in danger'. This I already knew.

She described how Isaac had somehow been lured into the darkness by two or three men. She again spoke of the initials of those involved. There, in the darkness, he was hit over the head, then dragged off. She said that he had been dragged twice. First to the riverbed 'where he was then killed', then dragged on to where

264

'the lions found him'.

She said that Isaac had information about 'something illegal' going on in that camp. Was anything stolen previously? I told her, somewhat astonished, about the rifle. 'It's not just that,' she continued. 'There's more. Precious stones, ivory, I think. Perhaps smuggling. There's more going on than what you think.' She then became unspecific. 'They are afraid that you know, while in fact you do not know, of everything. Or they think you will find out what is going on. You're like a policeman up there. You are always watching.'

I left her, incredulous at what I had heard. That she had said that Isaac had been dragged to the riverbed first, then further, was extraordinary. Isaac *had* been dragged to the river where blood and some of his clothing had been found. Then he had been dragged that considerable distance. Also, the fact that the rifle had been stolen was undeniable. I thought to myself, 'if the rest of what she described is as accurate, then the situation is more frightening and complex than we can imagine'. When

I thought of the smuggling aspect, I remembered a letter I had received a year earlier from a member of a vigilant UK-based animal lobbyist group. An extract from the letter reads as follows: 'Do you ever hear of ivory being moved out from Botswana to South Africa via the Tuli Block? I'm told there are lots of South African landowners there with airstrips on their land.' The big picture reveals that Botswana has for many years been a major route for ivory smugglers moving shipments into South Africa. In fact, one of the largest-ever seizures of ivory and rhino horn destined for South Africa occurred in October 1988 at the far northern Botswana borderpost of Kasangula.

In my opinion, it is not inconceivable that ivory has been smuggled into South Africa directly through the Tuli bushlands. For years, hundreds of Zimbabweans have crossed the bushlands from their country to illegally enter South Africa, normally under cover of darkness and much ivory, precious stones and drugs could have been ferried across.

The Zimbabweans enter South Africa

through a mysterious gap thirty-seven kilometres wide in the electrified 'incursion' military fence — erected by South Africa's previous government during the time of the armed struggle. The gap is directly adjacent to that section of the bushlands Limpopo river frontage. I have never been given a logical reason for the large gap in the middle of what would otherwise be a fiercely fortified fence which effectively divides South Africa from Zimbabwe and Botswana. Is it coincidence that the mysterious gap exists directly in front of border farms where it is alleged important cabinet ministers of the past regime regularly came to hunt wildlife and where *bosberaads* — political bush meetings — would be held? It is along this large gap where lions, like Batian, could have been lured to their deaths on the South African farms. For years, this mysterious gap has afforded easy access into South Africa for people. It would seem to be an ideal route for smugglers.

Actual ivory poaching has occurred in the Tuli bushlands for many years. I witnessed many of its horrors in the mid-1980s (just prior to the international termination of the ivory trade). At its peak, it was not uncommon to come across elephants, dying slow agonising deaths from the crippling bullets of AK47s. We would destroy the wounded. At other times, we found the poached carcasses, tusks removed and poachers long gone.

Early in 1993, ivory poaching flared up for a short time in the bushlands, then petered out quickly. Initially, I was surprised that it did not continue because the Tuli elephant population is vulnerable and relatively unprotected. The only real explanation I can give for the elephant poaching terminating so quickly is economic. The Convention on International Trade in Endangered Species (CITES) included the African elephant in its Appendix I listing and this dramatically reduced poaching and, more importantly, reduced ivory prices and its markets. Since the legal ivory trade's termination, apart from the flare-up just mentioned, Tuli elephants and other elephant populations have gained some security and to me, this is living proof of the effects of the Appendix I listing. But the situation is an uneasy truce. If legal trade is once again allowed, then the value of ivory will increase and this will increase poaching and ivory smuggling activities in places like Tuli.

However, not all smuggling has stopped. The smuggling of raw ivory from our part of eastern Botswana was uncovered in 1992 when the Endangered Species Protection Unit (ESPU) of the South African Police arrested three men from Selibe Phikwe, the largest town closest to the bushlands. The men were smuggling ivory to Johannesburg with their haul hidden in a tractor tyre. Also, in 1993, I was told that the brother of a friend of mine who once worked for the Charter Reserve was arrested in the northern Transvaal town of Pietersburg for being in possession of ivory (very probably from Tuli elephants). Is it coincidence, I wonder, that he was in Pietersburg with the ivory? I mention this as it has been said that illicit carving of ivory is taking place in Pietersburg. A Johannesburg-based Chinese man is believed to be moving ivory illegally from Swaziland

and Mozambique (and Botswana?) to his factory there.

One of the strangest and most suspicious cases of smuggling took place about eighteen months previously. It was reported to me that my anti-poaching team leader, Mafika, had shot and killed a South African border farmer in a smuggling affair. Alarmed and not believing this, I sought more information. I discovered that it was in fact thought to have been Mafika's brother who had been responsible for the killing.

It seemed that he was smuggling leopard skins across the border to sell to the farmer who, it was alleged, dealt in illicit ivory and skins. He crossed the border illegally and presented the skins to the farmer. Apparently, the farmer offered a low price. Whether Mafika's brother eventually took what was offered and handed the skins to the farmer, I do not know. But I was told that he returned to Botswana very angry. There was apparently already bad blood between them as the farmer was believed at times to shoot at Mafika's family's cattle if they strayed across the border. The brother then somehow came into possession of a rifle and returned to seek vengeance. I was told that he somehow entered the farmhouse undetected and shot the farmer dead, then seized a large amount of money from the farmhouse before crossing back into Botswana, where eventually he was apprehended by the police.

The details became shadowy, once the shooting was public knowledge. The strange part of this story is that subsequently, the incident was not, to my knowledge, reported in the South African press. This is strange because taking the political situation at the time into consideration, one would have imagined government-aligned newspapers willingly reporting on 'Border farmer murdered in farmhouse by Botswana assailant'. From a reliable government-related source in the northern Transvaal, I was told later, 'the press were kept out of it'. I wonder why? Who else might have been connected to the farmer and his alleged illicit dealings?

★ ★ ★

Was it possible that Isaac's death was related to such smuggling activities? In short, I could reply, 'Anything is possible in the Tuli bushlands when one considers its history.' To explain this reply, I need to paint a broader picture of the human influences on the bushlands, so that a more complete picture of aspects of the area's human personality emerges.

This portion of southern Africa, the adjoining border lands of these parts of Botswana, Zimbabwe and South Africa, has had much of its recent history swamped and shaped by human politics particularly during the era of institutionalised 'apartheid'.

Before that era, it was the Boers' aggression, their cattle rustling and threats to expand their Transvaal Republic further north and west into the bushlands and more that prompted King Khama to create a buffer state between him and the aggressor — this, in short, was how the Tuli Block was born. Cecil John Rhodes' Charter Company was granted this land concession of the border lands of Khama's country, but the concession was granted on condition that the land would be settled, creating a buffer with the neighbouring Boer Transvaal Republic.

In the 1940s, South Africa's government under General Jan Smuts proposed that the Tuli bushlands and the Transvaal lands should be the core of an international wildlife sanctuary. A scientific report had demonstrated that the land was unsuitable for agricultural purposes and that the area should be preserved 'for the recreation of the Nation'. The Dongola Wildlife Sanctuary Act was passed — but just prior to the forthcoming South African elections.

The National Party gained significant political support by backing the northern Transvaal's farming communities who opposed the new act. The National Party's ascendancy at this time marked the beginnings of environmental degradation in the bushlands and the Limpopo Valley. Once in power in 1948, they repealed the Dongola Wildlife Sanctuary Act. Smuts' vision was to be buried by politics and apartheid for the next half century and during this time, the land was hurt.

The newly-elected National Party,

ignoring the scientific report and its recommendations, proceeded to allocate this land adjacent to the Tuli bushlands to those farmers who supported their policies. In the 1980s, during the 'total onslaught' era, these farms were important — the government's 'frontline' with the 'black states' — a buffer through which insurgents first had to cross. The military presence along the border farms was great and most farmers belonged to a civilian commando and were given semi-automatic weapons by the Defence Force.

To the government securocrats, it was unimportant that the border farmers were growing irrigation-intensive crops and depleting the Limpopo's water table. Today, the Limpopo has been, in this stretch, reduced to an empty dry sand riverbed, only filling temporarily with the summer rains which are unpredictable anyway. The farming damaged habitat on both sides of the Limpopo. On the South African side, large tracts of pristine riverine bushland have been damaged by irrigation farming. Then, as the results of water-intensive farming methods took hold, magnificent riverine bush on the Botswana side began dying. Today, along some stretches, all that remains are graveyards of trees, the skeletal, fallen boughs and branches of riverine bush. The environmental damage is rooted in politics — and the damage has not been halted.

In addition, with the establishment of the De Beers' Venetia Diamond Mine, which is situated just beyond the buffer of border farms, it is feared that increased environmental damage will occur again as the Limpopo Valley is being used for man's needs — the water requirement of the diamond mine.

Returning to the years of the armed struggle, some South Africans working for landowners in the Botswana bushlands would feed information to the South African security on suspected insurgency movements and whatever else was going on in the bushlands. Such collusion was common. The South African security would also infiltrate the bushlands with 'informers' who, mainly amongst the Tuli populus, would glean information regarding freedom fighters and the whereabouts of ANC members and sympathisers.

I know of an occasion in the early 1980s when one South African working for a bushland landowner colluded with the South African security to secretly assist and enable them to cross undetected into the bushlands to investigate suspicions of an arms cache buried by freedom fighters near the Shashe/Limpopo river confluence. South African civilian 'spies' in Botswana aiding the apartheid government were at times uncovered and deported. Much was going on in those years and the local mood in the bushlands was understandably tense when the South African Defence Force (SADF) struck into Botswana's capital killing alleged ANC members — some of those killed were subsequently identified as having nothing to do with the ANC, but were Tswana members of the public. It was a strange time, with South Africa striking in Botswana and at the same time, South African tourists visiting the Botswana bushlands on safari in private South African-owned game reserves.

'South African poachers may trigger

border clash' read the bold headline in the South African *Sunday Times* at the end of 1990. The report highlighted again the 'South African' impact upon the Tuli bushlands. In the article, it was stated, 'A border clash is looming in the far northern Transvaal where South African hunters are illegally crossing the Limpopo to shoot game in the Tuli Block in Botswana.' Investigations began on reports that 'Hunters shoot game on the Botswana side of the river and drag the dead animals back into South Africa' and that 'Botswana (cattle) farmers live in fear of their families' lives during the hunting season with trigger-happy hunters on the South African side shooting at anything that moves'. In addition to this, I know of a case of a border farmer who actually shot dead one of his workers — claiming later that he had thought what he was aiming at was a baboon. Also in the article there were reports that South African helicopters 'are being used illegally to chase scores of game over the river into South Africa for wealthy overseas hunters to shoot'. The report went on to state 'South African farmers build tree houses for their clients at the river (the Limpopo) to take pot shots at animals coming down to drink' and that also they 'regularly put down baits at the tree houses to lure leopards towards the "hunters".'

I have witnessed some of these atrocities. Once, on an anti-poaching patrol, I discovered, with my Tswana team, South Africans firing fast and furious into herds of bushland antelope. We warded the poachers off and they ran back on to the South African riverbank. Quickly, I reported the matter to the South African Nature Conservation authorities and on this occasion, the culprits were found, arrested and charged.

Some of the border poaching has involved members of the South African Defence Force as the following story illustrates. In 1992, a Zimbabwean acquaintance of mine (who owns a substantial private game reserve several kilometres downstream from where the bushlands join Zimbabwe and South Africa) heard shots on his land near the Limpopo. Suspecting poaching, he ran to attempt to discover those responsible and apprehend them. Instead, it was he who was apprehended — by a group of SADF soldiers who were poaching on his land. The reserve owner was pushed on to his hands and knees, then forced in this position to cross into South Africa with them. They beat him with a radio aerial as they did this.

This incident, to my knowledge, did not become publicly known and, if it had been, it would have created embarrassment for the SADF. Could you imagine the headline? — 'Cross border poaching by SADF personnel who then abducted a Zimbabwean game farmer'. Instead, the incident did not become public and I heard later that an out-of-court settlement from the SADF to the Zimbabwean reserve owner was made.

★ ★ ★

In this chapter, I have told of much — of a clairvoyant's words about Isaac's murder, and connected smuggling, of my doubts that my lions were responsible for his death, of Isaac's case and my future.

I have also touched on the bushland intrigue, of the mysterious gap in the otherwise heavily fortified military border fence. I have told of ivory poaching in the bushlands, the smuggling of ivory from our part of Botswana and of cross-border smuggling of skins that resulted in human murder and suspected cover-ups.

I have also related how the past South African government's policy regarding the border farms has for over forty years (and still as I write) resulted in environmental degradation to the bushlands on both sides of the river. I wrote of how during the armed struggle, collusion between those in the South African security and the South African citizens working on the Botswana side existed. I have written of the South African hunters' illegal hunting atrocities in the bushlands and the case of SADF involvement in such activities . . . and there is more to be learnt at this story's end.

The Tuli bushlands is not a last eden, but a land that clearly has been tarnished by the crass, often cruel and criminal, actions of man. Knowing this, if one day Isaac's death was discovered to be linked to the issue of the stolen rifle and a cover-up of smuggling and other criminal activities, I would not be in the slightest bit surprised. This is what I suspect and I believe that ultimately the truth will one day be known.

12

The Golden Lost Souls

SOON it was December 1992 and another meeting was held between the Director, the manager and ourselves in Gaborone. The manager still wanted Rafiki to be held in an enclosure until a new reserve for her was found. I opposed this knowing how she, already traumatised, would react to being confined. The compromise agreement at the meeting was that I had to put an identification collar on her so that she could be recognised and, with baits, I had to try to keep her as close to my camp as possible.

Bophuthatswana National Parks' reserve, Pilanesberg, initially became an option for Rafiki's future. The management of Bop Parks had spoken to the Director about the possibility of both Rafiki and me moving to Pilanesberg. At that time, there was no lion population in the reserve.

Rafiki would not face opposition and I was granted permission to move Nelion with her. My role at Bop Parks would be to give publicity to the relocation of the last Adamson lion. Once settled, I would monitor Rafiki and Nelion's introduction and work towards further relocations of lions into Pilanesberg.

It then transpired that Pilanesberg would not be ready for a lion reintroduction programme until July 1993 — seven months later — as work on predator-proofing the 60,000 hectare reserve had only just begun. This put pressure on us as the Landowners' Association were attempting to put a deadline on the Department of Wildlife and myself by which to move Rafiki. At this time, I still faintly hoped that, if new information regarding Isaac's cause of death came to light, I would have justification for not moving her. This was a vain hope, of course, as whether Furaha had actually killed Isaac or not was not the issue.

Rafiki, at this time, was spending a lot of time with Nelion in the Tuli Safari area. Without her pride of Furaha, Sala and Tana with which to periodically join up, her movements were becoming influenced by Nelion. Most nights or early mornings, Julie and I would hear her and Nelion calling from the north. From tracks, I discovered that another lioness, possibly Nelion's sister, was in the area and it seemed increasingly possible that an alliance was forming with her and Rafiki.

From time to time, Rafiki would visit me at camp. Sadly on some occasions she still showed her anguish, but on the whole she seemed to be adapting gradually to her loss. I thanked God once again for her association with Nelion — and now too the developing relationship with the other lioness.

Christmas was approaching and our friend, Rozanne, visited us. She and Julie prepared a special Christmas lunch at Tawana. Rafiki appeared that evening and I went to spend some time with her as Julie and Rozanne remained hidden and quiet behind the hessian screening of the mess area.

My mood was at times extremely low. As Julie wrote to a friend at the time: 'The inevitable "lull" over the Christmas period has given Gareth time to dwell on his tragic loss. As a result, he is at present extremely depressed and disillusioned, finding it difficult to see any silver lining.' She continued, 'Our other problems, such as vehicles needing urgent repairs, financial worries etc. have only compounded Gareth's feelings of despair. I only hope that 1993 will be a better year and that Gareth's spirits will lift in time.'

Our daily diaries remained uncompleted with days and days of blank pages. The mourning had set in again. Julie and I felt, as we did at the time of Batian's death, as if we had lost an offspring. For some of the Christmas and New Year period, Julie left the bushlands to spend time in South Africa with her family. I remained in the bush and patrolled for poachers and their snares. During this time alone, though, some unusual writing was produced at new Tawana Camp.

One afternoon, I sat at the camp table in the mess. The shade temperatures were in the upper forties and as I sat there with a pad in front of me, I began writing prose. Words tumbled eagerly from me (in an atmosphere otherwise of heat and lethargy) and I did not feel that I was completely conscious and in control of the words. The pages filled, and 'Golden Lost Souls', as I later entitled the piece, was produced.

On its completion and as I read the words, it seemed that contained here was almost an anthem for the Lion Nation. The words encompassed lion life in true lion time. What I mean by this is that it first echoed the lions' age as a Nation, as a form of life older than man, and of the extent of their historical original ranges. It told of the lion cycle of life and death from conception, birth, development, sexual maturity, giving birth and then death . . . and life.

As the prose seemed to speak with a single voice representing all of its kind, the 'Lion Nation' tells of today, the vast reduction of its kingdom and how lions now die in many ways because of man. It tells of the bullets, the snares, the poison, the bullets again and it tells too of how man exploits 'Lion Kind' in captivity, the zoos and circuses. It tells of the effects of lion hunting and how, with the shooting of pride males by the hunters, the lion social system is torn apart. It ends with a message for man from the Lion Nation. It is published for the first time at the back of this book. The speed at which the prose was written staggered me, as did its length, and never have I experienced to the same extent such an uninterrupted flow of words. Changes to the verses were minimal and occurred only at the final verses — as it was there in the writing that the flow slowed and I began consciously thinking about the words.

Whatever its origins, it was written to be read — and hopefully understood for the betterment of the lion as I believe it creates an accessible insight into that Nation of Life. My hope for the 'Golden Lost Souls' writing is that it will be presented in pictorial book form and this is being worked upon. But here I have used the opportunity to have it read in the original form in which it was written.

In the bushlands, alone at a time of mourning, the words of 'Golden Lost Souls' became strangely comforting to me. I felt that whatever was to happen, in 'Golden Lost Souls' there was recorded the anthem of the Lion Nation and intermingled throughout were messages for man. I no longer felt a lone voice.

13

Facing the Planes of Timelessness

'WHY don't you just get out of the Tuli, then I am sure all this business about the lioness will die down?' These were the words of one of the Landowners' Association's committee members to me in January 1993. He was not speaking to me in his capacity as a committee member, but rather as an individual with an insight of the general mood within the Association. He was suggesting what he felt would be a solution to the matter. I do not think the Association would have formally agreed to leaving Rafiki alone if I left the area for a prolonged period. That after all, would be an admission that it was in fact my presence in the bushlands that was their problem.

For now, I knew it was imperative for Rafiki that I remain. Late in January, however, Julie and I reluctantly decided that a break, a week away at the South African coast, far from the bushlands with its day-to-day pressures, would be beneficial to us both. I was obviously uneasy about leaving, but with Julie's prompting, we left for our first break together for over three years. We left the pick-up in Johannesburg, and because of the generosity of an executive of Avis, we headed south towards the coast in a new and reliable Toyota sedan.

We could not really afford to do this, and spent six days in a small hotel right on the beach at what is known as the Dolphin Coast. During that time, we slept, swam, took long walks, but despite this, it was too early for the veils of pain and loss to be swept away. If anything, I dwelt even more on what had happened and the now uncertain future for Rafiki.

What I did not know then, or for that matter during most of our time together, was that the strain was perhaps even greater on Julie. My grief, anxieties and frustrations were in the open, but Julie, even during our time at the coast, held back and did not show her pain. She felt that if she had, it would make the situation worse for me. This highlighted the basic problem with our relationship. It was unequal in terms of emotional support. I needed support to succeed with my work and this she gave. Julie too needed support and I was usually too immersed in whatever situation or crisis to see this. Julie, for many different reasons, had to suppress a lot.

For that entire week, even as I watched dolphins every day streaking joyously through the waves of the ocean, my mind remained in the bushlands. The time passed quickly and soon we were back in the Tuli, heading along the rutted track towards camp. Julie was not to stay long. The clairvoyant's words about our safety still rang in my mind and I had suggested often to Julie that she consider leaving for a while. We had little money and she said she would go to take a job in Johannesburg which would help our situation in the bushlands.

Later that week, we had to spend a night in the northern Transvaal town of Messina, having gone there to get some urgently needed spare parts for the pick-up. Julie had planned to leave soon for Johannesburg and while in Messina we heard that a coach was expected, destined for Johannesburg, and it would be stopping early that morning. We made a quick decision, then collected her bags and she left.

Julie recently told me that as the coach drew away, she knew intuitively that she 'was not coming back' and, typical of Julie, that she 'felt bad leaving' me, feeling almost like a deserter. Over the weeks ahead, she did return on short visits and sometimes even for longer periods, but that morning in Messina, as she left waving to me, her time in the bushlands, with the lions, was over — and the final severing of our lives together had begun.

In the months ahead, Julie worked in Johannesburg, first for a safari agent, then as a researcher for a wildlife film company. It was only when she had been in Johannesburg for a while that she realised how 'burnt out' emotionally and physically she was. She sought the professional help of a psychologist who, because she was so emotionally traumatised, almost gave up on her. Julie sank to that grey level when life and death seem of no significance, the level at which the will to survive begins to leave. Thank God that with the passage of time, she began to heal and with this, she came to the realisation that she couldn't and wouldn't return to the trauma-plagued situation of the bushlands. We were in fact planning to be married later in the year and this too became another casualty of the situation in which we had found ourselves.

* * *

I now spent long periods alone in the bushlands and at night, was tormented by my fears and concerns. I am often asked if I was lonely during that time; I was alone, yes, but not lonely. There was so much going through my mind, and I was too focused upon the present to perceive the situation holistically and, unlike what Julie was discovering of herself and knew of me, I did not realise the effect that all the stress and trauma was having on me.

I do not think, however, that it was

paranoia that made me incredibly alert at night. I did take the clairvoyant's words seriously. Whenever I heard a vehicle driving through the bushlands at night, apparently in my direction, I would douse my candle, seize my shotgun and climb over the camp fence to hide in the darkness of the bush. The camp was not secure. In addition, the vehicles were unreliable and even the radio was faulty. I was relieved that Julie was in the safety of Johannesburg.

Each day in the late afternoon, I would build a small fire, prepare food (normally mopane worms, wild spinach or soya and rice) and while it cooked, I would wash my clothes, siphoning the water from the old 44–gallon drum. After that, I would eat hungrily, and then at twilight, I would always sit listening for Rafiki. When it was dark, I would take a candle and read in Julie's tent. I had moved out of mine beside the camp's fence as its position would have made me incredibly vulnerable if someone did want to attack me.

Later, I would fall asleep, but at the time, I would almost always wake up at the graveyard time of two or three in the morning. I would lie there awake, fuelled with fears and worries, and listening for suspicious sounds beyond the tent.

★ ★ ★

In the weeks ahead, to my relief, there was a lull in the calls for Rafiki to be moved. This was to be shattered in the third week of April after a news report of an elderly woman having been killed by a lioness in the grounds of an unfenced tourist lodge in the Phinda Resource Reserve in South Africa. The anger started up again and this incident was to have repercussions for Rafiki and my situation in the bushlands. Charges of culpable homicide were laid against the management of that private game reserve because it was thought that camp visitors were inadequately protected and that the situation could have been avoided. The reason why the calls for Rafiki to be removed became loud again was that if she killed a tourist in a similar unfenced private lodge in the bushlands, the management could also be charged

295

with culpable homicide — the situations would be identical.

The lady at Phinda had been walking along a path at night between the boma and her cottage. The lioness was nearby, allegedly hemmed in by the positioning of a wall and the swimming pool. The attack took place with the victim sustaining severe injuries to the calf, waist and neck. Tragically, she died later that night from shock and blood loss — dead on arrival after being flown to a hospital. The following day, the lioness with her two cubs were tracked down, darted, put in an enclosure and later shot.

News of this incident, in part because of the charges of culpable homicide laid against the lodge management, reverberated through the game lodge industry in South Africa. Most private lodges in South Africa are unfenced. I felt this tragedy would in turn prompt the fencing of lodges as well as other further precautions to better protect tourists.

The Phinda incident was widely reported and I remember one newspaper article which made the important point that it was game lodge management — not lions — who were responsible for tourist safety. As I said before, it seemed the rationale in the industry for South African lodges to be unfenced was that fences would detract from the 'bush ambience' created for the visitors. Tourists today are far more eco-conscious, and I feel would not wish to visit camps if they were unfenced for their perceived benefit and had the potential to bring humans and animals into fatal contact with each other. They would not want what was perceived by the industry to be their needs, i.e. 'bush ambience', to create a situation whereby wildlife was adversely affected.

In a *Weekend Telegraph* article entitled 'Born Free Lion at Centre of Safari Security Row', both arguments for and against fencing were discussed. The article ended:

> elsewhere in Africa, especially where the Big Five (elephant, buffalo, rhino, lion and leopard) occur, fencing is seen as essential to prevent people and animals stumbling into each other with fatal consequences

for both sides . . . Putting up more fences erects yet another barrier between ourselves and the wilds. But it is arguably the best way to avoid further tragedies, both human and animal.

In the bushlands, because it was perceived that Furaha was responsible for Isaac's death — and because of my previous warnings to the Landowners' Association of increased potential conflict due to the unfenced camps, I felt sure the Phinda incident would prompt fencing. Instead, to my disbelief, apart from a fence being erected at two staff compounds, the situation at camps and private lodges remained relatively unchanged. It still remains like this as I write and I feel inevitably one day an incident will occur at one of these camps — an incident which could have so easily been avoided.

Perhaps as a direct consequence of the Phinda incident, the Pilanesberg option for Rafiki fell through. I was told that Bop Parks personnel had decided to bring in an entire pride from elsewhere.

On hearing this, I spoke again with the Director, Nigel Hunter. He felt that now, there were only three options for Rafiki, none of which could remotely be described as good. The first would be to move her to a remote part of wild land in northern Botswana. There, poaching and hunting were rife, and apart from this, putting Rafiki into an area with an established lion population would cause untold stress and trauma for her. She would be treated by territorial prides as an intruder and trespasser and in turn would be harassed, if not killed, by them.

The second option was that a situation was created for her to remain in the bushlands, but Hunter stated that if she remained, he held great fears that someone would ultimately shoot her.

The third option was abhorrent to me — captivity. I said to Hunter that if the water situation and the need for fencing were addressed by the landowners, possible conflict with Rafiki and other potentially dangerous wild animals would be minimised, but Hunter had no authority to enforce the fencing issue with the landowners. I also suggested to him that if I established a waterpoint, by providing an engine for an existing old borehole pump in the Pitsani, in the core of Rafiki's range, this would lessen the chances of her and other predators being lured to waterholes at tourist and private camps. Hunter said that I should suggest these ideas to the manager.

This I did, accompanied by Charter warden, Bruce Petty. We expressed our thoughts to the manager. He in turn told us that for the foreseeable future, fencing would not be considered, that Rafiki must be removed and, if in the meantime we wished to establish a waterpoint on the Pitsani, that was up to us.

At this time, Rafiki was heavily pregnant and I told the manager that she couldn't possibly be moved in her condition, nor when the cubs were still very young. The trauma might cause her to abandon them. He provisionally agreed then that she should be removed when the cubs were six months old but this situation changed quickly in the time to come. I left his office depressed but at the same time determined to establish a waterpoint in the Pitsani Valley which would provide Rafiki, and hundreds of other animals, with alternative water and lessen the chances of her and other lions moving towards one of the tourist camps.

The following day, at 4.30 in the afternoon, Rafiki appeared at camp. She was exhausted, thirsty, hot and no longer pregnant. After she had drunk water, we greeted fondly for a long time. Later, she began heading down the hillside, stopping at intervals, calling, indicating clearly that she wished me to follow. She had done this before — after the birth of the stillborn cub and again after she had given birth to her previous litter. My lion daughter wished to lead me to her newborn.

Together we crossed the western plain, along the hills, before moving down towards Cub Koppie beneath which was the half-circle curve of the Tawana riverbed. We headed down to the riverbed, with Rafiki now leading the way. I knew that we were close to the nursery site. She now walked with caution, stopping at intervals, peering around for possible intruders and enemies such as leopard or hyaena who could pose a fatal threat to the defenceless newborns. She moved down the river bank, then called, and I saw them, side by side asleep in a hollow. I watched as they awoke to the sound which told them their mother was near. They were tiny, just twelve hours old I estimated, and they were unusually light in colour.

Rafiki had given birth once again in the Tawana Valley, this time south of the old camp, just a kilometre from her brother's grave. I sat upon the riverbank with mixed emotions as I watched her clean the squirming cubs. Occasionally, she would look up at me with knowing eyes.

One part of me felt elated. They were the beginnings of a new pride — the last having been taken away by man, leaving Rafiki alone. These were her and beautiful Nelion's little ones. Another part of me was depressed when my thoughts turned to both Rafiki's and now the cubs' uncertain future. I left the scene as soon as the sun was touching the horizon. I had to hurry back to camp. Twilight was seeping in as I headed back along the route we had come together. It was a route Rafiki and I were to get to know well in the days ahead.

On the first few evenings after the cubs' birth, I would help Rafiki by taking a container of water and a bowl to the nursery site. Initial nursing of cubs is intensive and apart from the water I provided at camp, it was otherwise scarce for miles around. Usually, if I found Rafiki with the cubs in the nursery, she would climb out of the hollow, stretch her stiff body, then come over to me — and greet me. I would pour water into the bowl and she would lap thirstily. On some occasions, she would remain where she was with the cubs, giving me a throaty greeting, then return to cleaning them or suckling them. On such occasions, I would stay awhile before burying the water container and the bowl in the gravel riverbed for the next day. I would then return to camp.

Those visits to Rafiki and the little ones were special private times. No one in the world knew where we were together. No one walked in the Tawana Valley and the few roads were reasonably well away. How I wished we could have remained like that, hidden in the bushlands, together . . .

Because of the pressure upon me, we — Rafiki, I and the little ones — almost did become eternally hidden. Not long after the birth of the cubs, I heard that Rafiki and the cubs might be moved to the captivity of a lion enclosure in Gaborone — and I knew that for Rafiki, this would be a fate worse than death. Rafiki was wild and free, having gained her priceless freedom which had been threatened twice before to be denied to her, and to Furaha and Batian; first with the death of their mother, and then with the murder of George. Here in the bushlands, I had enabled them to be free and for a third time, this seemed to be about to be taken from her. I could not tolerate this thought and was beginning to see no way out.

To protect Rafiki from what seemed then to be inevitable imprisonment, I feared that I would have to make the decision to take her life and those of her cubs just born into these wilds. How would I then feel? How could I live with myself after being driven to such a dire solution? How would I cope with the anger I would feel towards those responsible for forcing me to make that decision? I realised that all I would wish for would be to be with her, Furaha, Batian and the cubs in the plane of timelessness. I told myself that if I had to kill Rafiki and her cubs, I would take my own life too.

14

With my Soul Amongst Lions

AS I write, eighteen months have passed since that time of great despair. Fate dictated that the awful decision did not have to be made. I fought on for Rafiki and the cubs. First, I launched a publicity appeal for support for her which coincided with the screening on national television of 'Born to the Free', the documentary of the lions' story. The public's reaction to the documentary and media interviews was tremendous. People were enraged by the situation and offers of help streamed in. I was contacted by people throughout southern Africa — from Botswana, Namibia, Swaziland and Zimbabwe — and the telephone rang for days.

A journalist, clearly heated, sent me a fax saying, 'The whole situation is f-----g outrageous. Rafiki must be saved at any (all) costs. Please contact me.' An attorney offered her expertise and began to work towards gaining a court interdict to prevent Rafiki from being moved. The new owners of Tuli Safari Lodge sent a letter to me stating that they did not support the plan to remove Rafiki, as did others with interests in the bushlands, and these letters I sent to Nigel Hunter as proof that the decision had not been a unanimous one.

In addition, I sent a letter to the President of Botswana, Sir Quett Masire. I appealed to him on behalf of Rafiki, stating that she was the very last of the famous Adamson lions and that ultimately she belonged to the nation of Botswana. I also said that the story of the three — Batian, Furaha, and Rafiki — had given international publicity to the importance of the Botswana bushlands as a wildlife area. The Minister of Education, Ray Molomo (who was always a great supporter of my work), followed up my letter to the President by speaking to him personally on the matter. Ray felt strongly that Rafiki should not be removed from the bushlands, terming her as an important asset to the country.

During all this, I nevertheless had to continue seeking an alternative reserve for Rafiki and amongst the numerous faxes of support, there was one that introduced me to a developing wildlife region in South-east Zimbabwe called the Save Valley Conservancy.

In July, I travelled to Save Valley on a reconnaissance trip which was organised by the conservancy's chairman, Clive Stockil. I realised that Save had enormous potential. It comprises almost a million acres of bushveld which has been consolidated by its various landowners into a single conservancy. Save was an option for Rafiki and I appreciated the offer to settle her there. Once again, though, the opportunity fell through. The area was then still in the process of being completely fenced. Therefore, if Rafiki and the cubs were moved there, the lack of boundary fencing could have caused them to inadvertently enter the adjacent cattle country of the Tribal Trust lands. With this and other further complications, the Save option withered and died.

During the second week of July 1993, more bad news was received. One day, on my return from pumping water into the new waterhole that I had established on the Pitsani, I came across David Mupungu, warden of the neighbouring Tuli Safari Area in Zimbabwe. We had not seen each other for some time and although delighted to meet up, I quickly realised that David had an important issue to discuss. Frowning, he began telling me that a lioness had recently been illegally shot dead on his side of the bushlands and he feared it was Rafiki. He was driving along the Botswana/Zimbabwe border cutline that day hoping desperately that he might by chance come across me. I was shocked by the news, for a short time unable even to allow myself to react to what I was being told, that possibly Rafiki was dead.

He then told me the details. A hunter with a licence to shoot a leopard had allegedly mistaken the lioness for a leopard. He had hung an impala bait in a tree and was waiting hidden nearby when the lioness was attracted by the carcass. The hunter later said that the light was bad and he honestly thought she was a leopard. He therefore fired and killed her. David, the Zimbabwe Hunters Association and now I too, were furious at what he had done.

I knew that I now had to search for Rafiki. To contemplate her death was horrendous, and if it was her who had been shot, the cubs were hidden somewhere and would slowly starve if not found quickly. In the depths of my heart, I felt that Rafiki was not dead although this may just have been my refusal to accept that possibility. I went to the nursery site only to discover it empty — no sign of Rafiki or the cubs. I moved upstream towards the site of old Tawana Camp. The old camp consisted of the scant remains of two buildings and rubble. Most of the camp's fence poles had long before been pushed to the ground by elephants.

I walked into the old camp site, scanning the ground for signs. There, not three metres from where once my tent had been positioned, I saw Rafiki's spoor and that of the cubs. She had brought them here and hidden them in an old warthog burrow in what had been Julie's and my home for three years. She probably felt particularly secure leaving the cubs there due to her associations with the site. Further signs indicated that she had returned and taken the cubs elsewhere.

I was now almost completely sure that she was not the lioness shot so recently, but I needed to see her to confirm this as absolute. Therefore, in the afternoon of that same day, I drove with my friend Sam, caretaker of one of the private camps, to 'Rafiki's waterhole', where I had pumped water earlier, to check for signs and then to continue searching down the Pitsani Valley. Sam was to see a remarkable sight that afternoon.

We found no spoor at the waterhole, nor elsewhere in the valley. Returning, we decided to have one more look around the waterhole. Sam stopped the vehicle and as I stepped out, I saw immediately the very fresh tracks of a lioness. She had visited the waterhole just after we had first checked less than an hour earlier. Were they Rafiki's tracks?

I told Sam to stay in the vehicle while I investigated on foot. When I was about 150 metres from the vehicle, I thought

I heard a lion. I stopped, then, not hearing anything, continued on. About two minutes later, I heard Sam calling. I swung around and saw a lioness. Sam was shouting, 'Is this your lion, Gareth?' As he said that, I saw it was Rafiki. She was bounding towards me (although she did swerve when somewhat startled by Sam's yells). My heart could have burst with joy. She reached me, then leapt up on to her hind legs, hugged me briefly with her front paws on my shoulders, then returned to all fours. We greeted each other for many minutes, then sat together quietly. But from time to time she would look in the direction of the vehicle with suspicion and a little fear.

Later, I signalled to Sam that I would meet him on the border road above where we were. He started the vehicle and slowly motored away. When he had gone, I spent more time with Rafiki before eventually leaving her at sunset beside the waterhole. I walked away, feeling relieved and tired. Rafiki was safe.

With her cubs now increasingly mobile, I noticed that she was leading them frequently into the Zimbabwean Tuli Circle (Tuli Safari Area). She appeared to be ranging once again in the areas she had frequented with Nelion prior to the cubs' birth. Rafiki was safe, but which was the lioness who had been accidentally and tragically shot? The morning after I had found Rafiki, I met David at the Shashe river. As planned, he had brought the confiscated skin of the lioness for me to inspect. There upon the Shashe sands, he unfolded her skin. She had not in fact been an old female and I feared it was Nelion's sister.

In the weeks ahead, this fear was sadly confirmed as never again did I see Nelion's tracks with those of two lionesses. The killing, I discovered, had occurred in the heart of the country from which I would hear Nelion and Rafiki calling, and sadly this also indicated that it was indeed Nelion's sister who had been destroyed. It was a tragedy. Yet another Tuli lion gone — because of man.

★ ★ ★

Soon it was the end of July which marked the second anniversary of Batian's death. On the morning of the 29th, I walked across the hills and down to the Tawana Valley to the stone cairn I had built in his memory. As I walked up to the cairn, I inadvertently scattered an impala herd which had been feeding at this peaceful spot. After standing at the cairn, I sat beneath the nearby rain tree and thought of Batian. I thought that although he had been killed at the age of three, he had at least experienced more life in the wilds than poor Sala, Tana and the other cubs.

Sitting there, I tried to visualise how he would have looked that day if he had lived. Batian, at five years, would have developed from the husky young adult he had been into a fine large male still approaching his prime. Batian was always big for his age and would, I believe, have grown into one of the largest lions to have ever ranged in the bushlands.

As I sat there, I wished I could receive some sign from him. Later, I stood and walked back to the cairn.

Then, suddenly, I saw upon the dusty ground pawprints of a young male lion. It was amazing. I had passed the same spot as I had arrived, but had seen nothing. The size of the prints were the same as Batian's before his death. I then tracked and saw that the prints approached the cairn and then passed it. I followed — then I saw Batian's identification collar on the ground in front of me directly where the tracks led! I had put the collar in the hole in the rain tree approximately twenty months previously, and I had not seen it since. It had disappeared from the hole and I had presumed an elephant with a searching trunk had found it and strolled away with it. At the time of its disappearance, I had searched in the vicinity, but never saw it again — until then.

I had wished for a sign and that day, the second anniversary of Batian's death, I found tracks of a male lion which had led astonishingly to his collar. Strangely, on discovering the collar, I saw that it had been cut somehow. When I had hidden it in the tree all that time ago, it was buckled to form a circle and when I found it again, it lay out straight upon the ground.

I held the collar for a while, wondering what could possibly have caused the cut, and then returned it to the hole in the tree. Before leaving, I placed my hand, fingers outstretched, over the paw prints. As I walked away, tears touched my cheeks. Somehow Batian was with me.

★ ★ ★

One evening, just days before the anniversary of Batian's death, his rival in life, Zimmale, the male lion who had mated with Furaha and Rafiki months before, rose to his feet in the dark depths of the Shashe riverine bush. He shook his mighty head, yawned and began walking north parallel to the river. Zimmale was now in his prime, perhaps six years old, and had a thick and beautiful mane. He had resided in his Shashe kingdom for a year and a half. In that time, he had mated with the two lionesses with whom he had joined up and now four young lions carried his blood.

That evening, Zimmale was walking towards death. A double strand poacher's snare lay invisible in front of him, and he padded heavily towards it. The snare encircled first his head, then slipped and caught beneath his throat and around the nape of his neck. As Zimmale moved forward, the snare drew tight. He pulled backwards, not understanding the resistance he felt. Then he pulled to one side, but still he was held.

He pulled more, then fiercely thrashing, fighting, fighting, biting and clawing at all around him. He lashed out at low bushes, trampled flat the grass at his feet — and his loud growls shook the Shashe forests. He could no longer breathe in air, light in his mind was turning to dark and still straining at the wire, he slumped to the ground. A shrill whine vibrated from his soul, a whine that should haunt all that killed him — the poacher who laid the trap and those who did not provide protection for him.

His bladder emptied, his urine soaked

his hindquarters. Suddenly his pupils became wide. He died, crumpled, held by the wire.

When I heard the details of his death, an anger welled up within me such as I have never felt before. I burnt with rage. 'Zimmale is dead,' I screamed in my mind as I sat that night in my camp — and my heart is hot as I write this. His death was caused by poachers. His death could have been avoided. His blood is also on the hands of landowners — the people who have reprimanded me for speaking out on his kind's behalf, who tried to censor me. But they cannot censor this. I had warned for a long time that the future of the Tuli lions was in jeopardy, but I was told I was wrong. They would not listen — and now the last great pride master of the Tuli is gone.

The collage of photographs of snared victims which I have compiled for this book is grotesque, but I included these to record what has been allowed to happen to the once proud lions of the Tuli bushlands. Please turn to those pages. I wish for their pain to be felt, the manner of their deaths to be believed — particularly by those who contributed to the pain and to the deaths.

★ ★ ★

In August, I left the bushlands. Julie and I had planned to marry, but did not. In Johannesburg, Julie, now healing from the trauma of her life in the bushlands, realised she could not marry me. I understood. Marrying me would be marrying my pain and trauma. Much later, Julie wrote to me explaining how she had felt:

> I had suddenly become really scared. Something in me said 'Gareth plus lions plus Tuli equals Trauma equals Gareth'. It became almost as if you were the personification of all the trauma and pain we experienced in the Tuli. I now realise how totally mixed up things had become at that time ... I'd say that we were two people who could, under different circumstances, have really

complemented each other . . . What-ever, we had, and even apart still have, a special relationship.

My mother had offered to fly us both to England so that she could meet Julie for the first time. I phoned her to tell her that Julie and I were no longer to marry and asked her if she still wished us to go to England. She did. We went together, but on our return, I headed north to the bushlands and Julie went south to a position in a Natal game reserve.

As time passed, I began spending less and less time in the bushlands. My absence meant emphasis was taken off Rafiki. Rafiki's cubs were growing up not knowing me, their mother's friend. Even during the period when I did return to the bushlands, I saw her infrequently. With the cubs mobile, she was now fortunately shifting her range out of the Tawana and Pitsani Valleys in Botswana and increasingly roamed Nelion's range in the Zimbabwe Tuli Safari Area. There they belong to the Zimbabwe nation and are protected in the land under warden David Mupungu's guardianship. Lastly, and most importantly, she was protected from the landowners and their calls for her to be moved — and once again, I thanked God for Nelion.

★ ★ ★

Towards the end of the year, as the first anniversary of the deaths of Isaac, Furaha, Sala and Tana came and passed, dark dealings and dark allegations were occurring. The wife of the game ranger who had first come across Isaac's body was (with another family member) caught and convicted for attempting to sell elephant tusks in the northern Transvaal — caught by an undercover member of the Endangered Species Protection Unit (ESPU) of the South African Police. She and her partner in crime were fined R10,000 each. In the same month, the headmaster of a school west of the Tuli bushlands was also caught attempting to sell elephant tusks. I was told that he too was found guilty and was sentenced to ten years imprisonment. Was there a link between the two cases . . . and a link to much more?

Only a month later, I received some startling information concerning Isaac's death. An informant of mine, whose identity I must continue to protect, came to my friend, Bane Sesa, with the following information. He told him that a staff member at the same camp at which Isaac worked had come to him and had told him in confidence that Isaac was not killed by the lions! He recounted that he had been murdered, then left in the bush in the certain knowledge that his body would be found by the scavengers — ultimately the lions. His alleged description of events was chillingly similar to that of the clairvoyant.

On hearing this, Sesa and I contacted the CID with what we had learnt. We both felt we had made a breakthrough and that the truth of what had really happened on the night of the 29th October was closer to being revealed than ever. The CID gratefully received the information, but afterwards we heard little of their investigation. Perhaps this was because no third party had heard the conversation between the man and our informant. Thus the conversation in reality could simply be denied by the man so as to cover up the truth. The same could apply to our informant — out of fear. It was at this time that Isaac's brother, Solomon, unexpectedly told me something strange. Solomon had worked for the same safari company as his brother, but had left as he was afraid after Isaac's death. Over the months, I had spent time with him and his and Isaac's family discussing the case. We had agreed that foul play — murder — was possible.

Out of the blue, when discussing with me what our informant had revealed, he told me that the doctor who had examined Isaac's body had written on the hospital form that Isaac had not been killed by lions.

Later in the week, I was staggered to read of the following in the final pages of Adrian House's newly published biography on George and Joy Adamson entitled, *The Great Safari*. Adrian wrote about how Furaha had 'met a bizarre end'. He told how a tracker's body was found mauled near where Furaha was with the cubs. He wrote about how she was shot 'before a post-mortem was carried out on the tracker' — and that two months later, 'the doctor reported that the man had been killed by a bullet, and his body eaten not by a lion, but a hyaena'. It was hard to know how to react to this and I contacted Adrian, who I know, to ask him where he had sourced this information. The part about the doctor reporting two months later that the lions were not responsible seemed very specific.

Adrian told me he would check through his notes and later, in a letter, he replied that he was unable to find the exact source, but felt he had either read the information in a newspaper report, or it had been given to him while he had been researching for the book in Africa.

I later had a meeting with the local head of the CID about this and other information that had come to light. I learnt that the doctor was no longer in the country (he had been an expatriate) as his contract had expired, and he had returned to Zambia.

The post-mortem report was to me the single most grey area in the case.

The post-mortem should have been undertaken before my lions were shot, and in the actual report, as I have previously mentioned, the cause of Isaac's death was not stated. It did not specifically say in which manner or from what Isaac died. If the lions had been human and tried in a court of law, this and general lack of evidence would have maintained, I feel, that they would not have been sentenced to death.

Before leaving the meeting with the head of the CID, I was assured that the information would be investigated further and that the doctor would probably be contacted. But it seems the wheels of the investigation were turning slowly — perhaps deceptively so.

As I write, the case remains open and unsolved. Many questions remained unanswered. But as I have already written, I believe one day the truth will come to light — what could be dismissed as 'speculation' today could be unmasked as 'reality' tomorrow.

★ ★ ★

On occasions, while writing this book, I have visited the bushlands to seek signs of Rafiki and the cubs — to be reassured that all is well. I no longer seek physical contact with her. I deny us, two beings species apart but once of one pride, our fellowship. Her cubs are eighteen months old, hunting, playing and resting with their mother in the bushlands.

Recently, on a visit, I stood beside the waterhole at the quiet place right on the border of Botswana and Zimbabwe. The water shimmered, its levels restored by the past good season of rain — a marvellous contrast to the previous years of drought. Imprinted on the soft soil at my feet were Rafiki's pawprints and those of her cubs. They had drunk at this place just a few hours before. Vultures circled in the sky above me. Rafiki was on a kill not far from where I stood, but was hidden by the bushlands. Neither of us could see the other, but I felt the connection. We were meeting with our hearts, our spirits touching again.

Standing there alone in the midst of the bushlands, I then thought of Batian, Furaha, Sala and Tana. With

326

all their images flickering like portions of a constantly changing collage in my mind, I spoke to them too, saying softly as the breeze caressed my face, 'How I wish you were here.'

As I write these words, I think of Julie. I think of her commitment to the lions, her support to me, and the love she gave to us all — and we thank her, and love her.

She wrote the following words some time after we parted, words that are the early roots of the story she too will tell one day:

Gareth has chosen a path which I can only admire. I hope that I may walk a parallel path — though admittedly I do so with trepidation. I am scared for Gareth as he too must be scared — though for those he has chosen to represent. Lions are the focus of Gareth's life and it is the dangers facing lions which Gareth too faces.

Towards the end of 1994, when much of this book was written, I began to return to the bushlands periodically. Tragically, my friend, Alpheus Marupane has a terminal illness and I would visit him and his family, staying with them where they live at a camp on the Limpopo. Whenever I was in the bushlands at that time, I would feel uneasy. Alpheus' condition was obviously one of the reasons for this. I am frustrated and become saddened that so little can apparently be done for him, a man who was always there for me during troubled times. He, a brave man, fights his illness head-on and the fact that he is still alive as I write is an extraordinary testament to the resilience of the human spirit. He refuses to give up. Another reason for my unease rests with the unknown, of what I still do not know surrounding the case of Isaac and my lions.

There are enemies out there in the bushlands and beyond. Recently I pondered on what could have occurred if I had remained at Tawana to write this book instead of (wisely) moving south to concentrate upon it and to begin to restore and heal myself. For all that time away, Tawana Camp stood alone and hollow, day and night, apart from during my short visits through the year. It stood there for all that time, the ghost camp that it is; a lonely camp of the ghosts of my past, my lions. The old tents shook with the wind, were blasted by the sun and then rain came, hurling down upon the canvas, the mess hut's roof and all around. The weaver birds then came as usual to build their nests and to breed.

Earlier in the year, I had removed from the camp most of the important diaries, reports, articles and those papers which in part have made up this book. I also took most of my few valuable possessions.

And so it stood. Tawana, unentered and untouched by man, a ragged memorial to five years of life with lions in the bushlands. Then, at the very end of the year, ten months later, at a time when it would have been known that I was in the area, a time when I was visiting Alpheus, people came to Tawana. I do not know who they were. They entered the camp and ransacked the place, rifled through piles of books, papers and other possessions under canvas and in cupboards, spilling them on to the bare ground.

Both my small dome tents were violently slashed open with knives. Possessions of mine were taken — but an expensive video camera battery charger (which I had forgotten to remove previously) was not. It was placed strangely and conspicuously on top of the ash pile beside which I would cook food. I discovered too a leather holdall containing papers placed equally strangely inside one of the lions' empty water containers outside the camp. I wonder why they did this?

Alone, on the very last day of 1994, in the last light of that day, I discovered all this. Tawana had been trashed. Yes, I was shocked initially, but not for long. Nor was I intimidated much. Hurt? No, I am beyond that now as greater hurt has left me hardened today. At the dawn of the new year's day, I began to tidy the damage done, starting this year clearing up and picking up the pieces of my past, the strewn letters, old manuscripts and photographs.

In another sense, this is how I am embarking upon this new year — picking up the pieces, refusing to be drowned by the past. In the past year, I admit that at times I was almost lost completely to my sadness. As Julie had experienced, I too sank to that grey level where life and death seem of no significance, that level where the will begins to leave one.

Now, with renewed hope and strength, I will be letting myself go forward again, to embark upon a new chapter — with my soul amongst lions. The tides in the Tuli are due to turn one day. Like my friend Alpheus with his life, I am not giving up on life, lion life or the lives of lions.

I end this tale with words of necessary painful departure to new beginnings:

But as he descended the hill, a sadness came upon him and he thought in his heart:
How shall I go in peace and without sorrow?
Nay, not without a wound in the spirit shall I leave . . . long were the days of pain . . . and long were the nights of

aloneness, and who can depart from his pain and his aloneness without regret? Too many fragments of the spirit have I scattered . . . and too many are the children of my longing that walk naked amongst these hills, and I cannot withdraw from them without a burden and an ache.

It is not a garment I cast off this day, but a skin that I tear with my own hands.

Nor is it a thought I leave behind me, but a heart made sweet with hunger and with thirst.

Yet I cannot tarry longer.
The sea that calls all things unto her calls me,
And I must embark . . .

The Prophet — Kahlil Gibran

Final Note

The Future of the Tuli Bushlands
— The International Peace Park Initiative

The first democratic elections in South Africa have taken place, the previously suppressed majority has spoken. South Africa, and in fact the entire southern African sub-region, has entered a new era, a new era of peace we pray. Soon the Botswana Tuli bushlands could become the heart of a symbolic Peace Park, linking up with large portions of wilderness in Zimbabwe and South Africa. Initiatives are taking place for the ecologically debilitating agricultural border farms and game farms south of the bushlands to be developed into a South African game park. If this comes about, the thirty-seven-kilometre gap in the incursion fence would suddenly become irrelevant. In fact, the incursion fence itself could be brought down to create a natural, open, fenceless boundary between the bushlands and the new wildlife park. That fence, erected by the apartheid government, the ownership of those border farms, the land utilisation which has taken place — they all belong to the past, to the political past which bore them.

The Peace Park initiative would allow wildlife from the Botswana bushlands and the Zimbabwe Tuli Safari Area free movement, as it was in the historical past, into a former portion of their natural range. Lions could move south into the northern Transvaal, with no fear of being shot, there would be no more cross-border poaching and habitat would be reclaimed for the original wild denizens. Through the wildlife of three countries, the new South Africa would then be part of the whole. The criss-crossing of wild animals across once tense human boundaries would symbolise the end of the past South African isolation from the rest of Africa.

This is my dream, the dream of many. The strong symbolism of a Southern African Peace Park would focus much international attention and in turn attract visitors to a region where wild animals walk unrestricted across portions of three African countries.

The creation of a South African Park to adjoin the Tuli bushlands would put great emphasis on the need for greater preservation on the Botswana side. The 'whole', the international Peace Park, would only be ecologically sound if all three of its components are conserved diligently. The landowners on the Botswana side would have to afford protection for the animals and the land. The bushlands needs a warden to be appointed and game scouts trained and deployed to undertake stringent anti-poaching across all the private reserves. Or, perhaps because of the international significance of a Peace Park, the Botswana government may step forward and, through its Wildlife Department, initiate, with the landowners, a conservation plan for the bushlands compatible with wildlife policy in the new Park and north in Zimbabwe. Land ownership could remain as it is, but the implementation of a conservation plan could fall under the Wildlife Department and a Trust Fund could be established with money from donors being put to use for wildlife preservation in the bushlands — the government's contribution to the spirit of the Peace Park.

For example, a simple tariff payable to the Trust by all visitors would in a short time raise important wildlife funding at little or no outlay cost. Local people and the wildlife could benefit by, for example, the Trust establishing a cultural craft co-operative market situation near the border post through which the tourists enter the bushlands. Tourists entering or leaving could visit the market, with a percentage of whatever sale is made being set aside for conservation.

If lions are to be a viable species in the overall Peace Park, not only must poaching be clamped down upon, but the bushlands' western boundary — the government's veterinary cordon fence — would have to be predator-proofed in its entirety, thus preventing lions from killing the livestock of the local people and in turn preventing lions from being killed in retaliation. The success of the initiative would depend upon continual cross-border conservation consultation and discussion in terms of decision-making taking place between the local peoples of that corner of South Africa, Botswana and Zimbabwe.

The Peace Park must become a reality soon if a great number of Tuli elephants are to be saved from a very real threat. For several years now, the Landowners' Association has been working towards 'utilising' Tuli elephants to bring in finance. Despite the fact that no elephant research ever undertaken in the bushlands has concluded that the area cannot sustain the existing elephant population, this is thought otherwise by a core of the owners — who, incidentally, have no academic grounding related to elephant ecology.

They wish to sell 100 or more elephants at R10,000 each to buyers in South Africa such as De Beers who own the Venetia Reserve fifteen kilometres south of the bushlands. I vehemently oppose this proposal for many reasons, and I am not alone. Some of the landowners claim there are too many elephants for the area (which is unproven), but with the creation of the Peace Park, this argument will fall away as habitat will be substantially increased and a reduction will be unnecessary.

But despite the Peace Park initiative, the selling of Tuli elephants is still being promoted, indicating that its justification is economic as opposed to ecological. A recent advertisement reads 'Adult Elephants for Sale — No limitations'. I later discovered this meant that any elephant bought from the Tuli bushlands could then be hunted and shot. Conservation is a dirty game. If this sale of elephants takes place, just as these great herds are about to regain another portion of their ancestral range, many of them could be sold and shot. Time will tell whether the Peace Park loses a portion of its most valuable asset, the elephants, before it is even formed.

Today, the integration of former freedom fighters into the new South African Defence Force is taking place. These men and women, who fought for the liberation of their country, could use their skills to serve and protect and provide liberty for the wildlife of the Peace Park. So too could real jobs be created, through eco-tourism, for those poor Zimbabwean men and women currently earning slave wages on the South African border farms.

I believe the Peace Park initiative could be the light at the end of a very long dark tunnel for the wildlife in the bushlands. The lions, the elephants and all the wild denizens of this land may have been whispering for years, 'Is this my soul's land? — or just soil to cover my bones?'

Golden Lost Souls

We the lions of the past,
Today's ghosts,
Roamed endless plain and wide
mountain range
Before man became man, before
Man stood upright, peering with curious
eyes —
Fuelled by a mind that in time destroyed
much. Man
Today, it seems destined, will destroy that
Very same one with curious eyes and mind
Who rose upright from the plains.

Us, ghosts today, the lions of the past
Lived throughout much of this ancient
continent, Africa
And beyond.
From harsh mountain range north at
night caressed by winds
From where the blue meets the blue,
The forests' dark depths

And eastern plains dotted with our
abundant prey,
Decorating the land like a moving mosaic
of flowers.

We, the children of the lions of olden
times
On these same eastern plains
Were born within grassy gulleys
And within bushy banks of streams.
Secret nursery places chosen with care
By our mothers.

Life in the beginning for us children
of the lions
Was an unclear place of shapes.
Some dark, some light, as we peered
With barely opened eyes.
Our golden mother's tongue,
again and again
Would clean our spotted backs
And we,
The children of the lions, would
Clamber about on unsteady legs.
Our golden mother would protect us
as best she could —
But some of us died,
Killed by leopard, hyaena or by fierce

other golden fathers,
Having chased away our own.

We would grow, taste meat for the
first time
And tumble, tumble, tumble
Upon grassy endless plains.
Our childhood is long, a learning time,
Learning from our golden mothers, aunts
and benign golden
Fathers.
Always togetherness in our golden lion
families,
Making us lions.

We would, as children of lions, learn
to hunt with the family.
In time be the one who seized those
Of stripes, those with horns, those we
must kill
To in turn enable us to live.
Our urge to kill is not fuelled by a
malevolence, or hate
But by a spirit to live, a spirit of life.

Feast, then days of fast,
The pendulum constantly alternating
With the rhythm of the seasons

and migrations.
We, with seasons passing, we the children
of the lion
Feel the change within us,
no longer children,
Then copulate for days — then stop.
One day we would enter that
grassy gulley
Or that bushy bank by the stream
In which we too had been born,
To give birth to children of the lion of
our own
We would do as our golden mother did,
Caring, protecting,
Raising beloved children of
the lion under
An African sun and staring moon.

With these children grown, with now
Our own mothers, old golden mothers,
Again we would give birth, to care, to
teach and hunt
With more beloved children of the lion,
until
We too became old golden mothers.

In that time the children of the lions
are the ones we are dependent upon,

Dependent upon their hunts,
Their care.
We, with teeth now worn, weary eyes,
loose bellies
and creaking backs,
Walk within the family with new golden
fathers,
New tumbling children of the lions on
endless plains.

Like a great setting golden sun
We too reached our own farthest horizon
and
Life slips away
Leaving golden forms to be consumed,
To give life to others of the African
plain,
and those of the sky blue — an exchange
of life.
Simple.
We, the old golden ones, would leave
behind
Our living, tumbling, hunting, caring,
copulating,
Fighting, feasting legacy.
We would be content golden ghosts of
endless plains
Remembered by our ancestors in heaven.

Today the pads of our feet
no longer walk
Forever endless plains, mountain
range wide.
We live in pockets of land, no longer free
spirits.
Like many of the old wilds, we now live
in twilight times.
We are born in the twilight of
the life of lions —
Our life is much altered.

Some of we children of the lion
Die before we are born into that twilight.
A bullet may crash into a
golden mother's head,
Then another into where we lie within
her — unborn.
Men then appear, gloat and stand above
the golden mother's
body,
Us, within her, dying unborn,
And with sweaty faces, the men smile.

We die as wire traps encircle our necks.
The wire tightens, we fight.
The wire eats into our golden fur
Then into red flesh, choking us.

The light turns to red, blood red,
Then before our eyes there is only
Black.

Man will again appear as our
Spirits watch from secret shadows,
Us watching our dead, crumpled, gold
Forms.
Man then strips our gold from our
bodies
And then we are left,
Our spirits watching the grotesque red
Forms, us.
The bloated eyes, protruding, but unseeing.
Us.

Children of the lion tumble on
restricted plains
When golden mother falls dead after the
crash,
Another bullet, another death.
Children of the lion run terrified
to nowhere,
Then wait for their mother's return
Only she never returns.

The children of the lion no longer tumble
but lie

347

forlorn,
Now less their golden mothers,
And wait and wait till we, the bone
jutting, tawny
Children of the lion
die,
Here, there, almost everywhere
Where lions can still walk upon pockets
of plain,
Forest depths, mountain range.

We lions die living, die eating.
We kill a cow, the cow kills us.
Its flesh will be anointed by man
with poison.
We feast, our stomachs writhe like snakes
in pits of coals.
We vomit, we defecate, retching, shitting,
Then die with our excrement around us,
on us.
Others come to eat — the chain of life
needs to continue.
But
The links are eroded by the poison.

The jackal moves away from the circles
of excrement
Around us,

and
Vomits and shits.
The vulture rises into the sky to feel the
thermals,
Then sinks, madly flapping, flapping in
its madness
Before hitting the ground.
It shits, vomits
and dies.

The hyaena by night lopes forward,
Biting and swallowing what he finds,
Then slinks away to rest.
The raging thirst begins, then the raging
madness
Of pain.
He dies alone on the plain.

Children of the lion are today in
Some places bred by man,
And man delionises the children, humiliates
The children to make them perform
feats in
Front of crowds and crowds of watching,
Laughing, squealing, shouting people.

After the tricks, the children are prodded
into small cages to await the next time.

What misery, what despair as the
children of the
Lion stare with unblinking amber eyes
Out into a changed world,
Head resting on paw, cramped within
a cage.
Now sad, a sad, sad facsimile of his
proud ancestors
of endless plains, forest depths, mountain
range.

Man has taken our land.
He destroyed what we are dependent
upon —
The other old ones, the denizens of a
shrinking,
Ancient world,
Those of stripes, those with horns, those
we must kill
To enable ourselves to live.

Man will kill us with mad malevolence
Lusting particularly to kill the
golden fathers
with their fine heads.
We, the family, shout our anger
After man shoots the golden father dead.
As droplets of his rich blood drip onto

sand, leaf or stone,
We flee.
Without our golden father, the security
he gave,
We flee.

Fierce fathers come in time to take his
place
And children of the golden father in turn
are killed.
Our society becomes unbalanced.
A new golden father is tolerated by
Golden mothers and aunts as time passes.
They copulate and new children of
the lions
arrive.
They grow . . .

Then man comes again seeking golden
fathers
The new is murdered like the old.
We shout our anger,
Drip, drip, rich blood on sand,
leaf or stone.
We flee.
Our society is torn apart
and will happen again.
Imbalance.

351

A man kills a lion. To man this is
acceptable.
A lion kills a man?
'Kill it! Kill it! Kill it!'
scream other men
and another golden father dies,
Another golden mother dies,
With us, the unborn, within her.

We are not your underlings, man.
We are another nation of life,
Old, old, nation of life to whom
the land belongs.
And you
are destroying that from which
You could ultimately learn.

We walked the endless plains long before
you
Walked upright and became man.
We are of an old, polished life,
old life,
Lion life of ancient times.

Think of your unborn man, and their
unborn.
Think about the world you have carved
up, poisoned.

352

Think about the children of lions
on the restricted plain.

What you are doing to the lion
You unwittingly — you with curious
Eyes and minds —
Are doing the same unto yourself —
Ripping the umbilical cord of your nation
Your kind
From this earth.

TO FIGHT THE WILD
Rod Ansell and Rachel Percy

Lost in uncharted Australian bush, Rod Ansell survived by hunting and trapping wild animals, improvising shelter and using all the bushman's skills he knew.

COROMANDEL
Pat Barr

India in the 1830s is a hot, uncomfortable place, where the East India Company still rules. Amelia and her new husband find themselves caught up in the animosities which seethe between the old order and the new.

THE SMALL PARTY
Lillian Beckwith

A frightening journey to safety begins for Ruth and her small party as their island is caught up in the dangers of armed insurrection.

THE WILDERNESS WALK
Sheila Bishop

Stifling unpleasant memories of a misbegotten romance in Cleave with Lord Francis Aubrey, Lavinia goes on holiday there with her sister. The two women are thrust into a romantic intrigue involving none other than Lord Francis.

THE RELUCTANT GUEST
Rosalind Brett

Ann Calvert went to spend a month on a South African farm with Theo Borland and his sister. They both proved to be different from her first idea of them, and there was Storr Peterson — the most disturbing man she had ever met.

ONE ENCHANTED SUMMER
Anne Tedlock Brooks

A tale of mystery and romance and a girl who found both during one enchanted summer.

CLOUD OVER MALVERTON
Nancy Buckingham

Dulcie soon realises that something is seriously wrong at Malverton, and when violence strikes she is horrified to find herself under suspicion of murder.

AFTER THOUGHTS
Max Bygraves

The Cockney entertainer tells stories of his East End childhood, of his RAF days, and his post-war showbusiness successes and friendships with fellow comedians.

MOONLIGHT
AND MARCH ROSES
D. Y. Cameron

Lynn's search to trace a missing girl takes her to Spain, where she meets Clive Hendon. While untangling the situation, she untangles her emotions and decides on her own future.

NURSE ALICE IN LOVE
Theresa Charles

Accepting the post of nurse to little Fernie Sherrod, Alice Everton could not guess at the romance, suspense and danger which lay ahead at the Sherrod's isolated estate.

POIROT INVESTIGATES
Agatha Christie

Two things bind these eleven stories together — the brilliance and uncanny skill of the diminutive Belgian detective, and the stupidity of his Watson-like partner, Captain Hastings.

LET LOOSE THE TIGERS
Josephine Cox

Queenie promised to find the long-lost son of the frail, elderly murderess, Hannah Jason. But her enquiries threatened to unlock the cage where crucial secrets had long been held captive.

THE TWILIGHT MAN
Frank Gruber

Jim Rand lives alone in the California desert awaiting death. Into his hermit existence comes a teenage girl who blows both his past and his brief future wide open.

DOG IN THE DARK
Gerald Hammond

Jim Cunningham breeds and trains gun dogs, and his antagonism towards the devotees of show spaniels earns him many enemies. So when one of them is found murdered, the police are on his doorstep within hours.

THE RED KNIGHT
Geoffrey Moxon

When he finds himself a pawn on the chessboard of international espionage with his family in constant danger, Guy Trent becomes embroiled in moves and countermoves which may mean life or death for Western scientists.

TIGER TIGER
Frank Ryan

A young man involved in drugs is found murdered. This is the first event which will draw Detective Inspector Sandy Woodings into a whirlpool of murder and deceit.

CAROLINE MINUSCULE
Andrew Taylor

Caroline Minuscule, a medieval script, is the first clue to the whereabouts of a cache of diamonds. The search becomes a deadly kind of fairy story in which several murders have an other-worldly quality.

LONG CHAIN OF DEATH
Sarah Wolf

During the Second World War four American teenagers from the same town join the Army together. Forty-two years later, the son of one of the soldiers realises that someone is systematically wiping out the families of the four men.

THE LISTERDALE MYSTERY
Agatha Christie

Twelve short stories ranging from the light-hearted to the macabre, diverse mysteries ingeniously and plausibly contrived and convincingly unravelled.

TO BE LOVED
Lynne Collins

Andrew married the woman he had always loved despite the knowledge that Sarah married him for reasons of her own. So much heartache could have been avoided if only he had known how vital it was to be loved.

ACCUSED NURSE
Jane Converse

Paula found herself accused of a crime which could cost her her job, her nurse's reputation, and even the man she loved, unless the truth came to light.

CHATEAU OF FLOWERS
Margaret Rome

Alain, Comte de Treville needed a wife to look after him, and Fleur went into marriage on a business basis only, hoping that eventually he would come to trust and care for her.

CRISS-CROSS
Alan Scholefield

As her ex-husband had succeeded in kidnapping their young daughter once, Jane was determined to take her safely back to England. But all too soon Jane is caught up in a new web of intrigue.

DEAD BY MORNING
Dorothy Simpson

Leo Martindale's body was discovered outside the gates of his ancestral home. Is it, as Inspector Thanet begins to suspect, murder?

A GREAT DELIVERANCE
Elizabeth George

Into the web of old houses and secrets of Keldale Valley comes Scotland Yard Inspector Thomas Lynley and his assistant to solve a particularly savage murder.

'E' IS FOR EVIDENCE
Sue Grafton

Kinsey Millhone was bogged down on a warehouse fire claim. It came as something of a shock when she was accused of being on the take. She'd been set up. Now she had a new client — herself.

A FAMILY OUTING IN AFRICA
Charles Hampton and Janie Hampton

A tale of a young family's journey through Central Africa by bus, train, river boat, lorry, wooden bicycle and foot.

THE PLEASURES OF AGE
Robert Morley

The author, British stage and screen star, now eighty, is enjoying the pleasures of age. He has drawn on his experiences to write this witty, entertaining and informative book.

THE VINEGAR SEED
Maureen Peters

The first book in a trilogy which follows the exploits of two sisters who leave Ireland in 1861 to seek their fortune in England.

A VERY PAROCHIAL MURDER
John Wainwright

A mugging in the genteel seaside town turned to murder when the victim died. Then the body of a young tearaway is washed ashore and Detective Inspector Lyle is determined that a second killing will not go unpunished.

DEATH ON A HOT SUMMER NIGHT
Anne Infante

Micky Douglas is either accident-prone or someone is trying to kill him. He finds himself caught in a desperate race to save his ex-wife and others from a ruthless gang.

HOLD DOWN A SHADOW
Geoffrey Jenkins

Maluti Rider, with the help of four of the world's most wanted men, is determined to destroy the Katse Dam and release a killer flood.

THAT NICE MISS SMITH
Nigel Morland

A reconstruction and reassessment of the trial in 1857 of Madeleine Smith, who was acquitted by a verdict of Not Proven of poisoning her lover, Emile L'Angelier.